TOM +

~THE

"MACHATONEM"

WITH LOVE

Barba

How To Succeed In Business By Busting Your Ass

Irving Zeiger

Bloomington, IN   Milton Keynes, UK

AuthorHouse™
1663 Liberty Drive, Suite 200
Bloomington, IN 47403
www.authorhouse.com
Phone: 1-800-839-8640

AuthorHouse™ UK Ltd.
500 Avebury Boulevard
Central Milton Keynes, MK9 2BE
www.authorhouse.co.uk
Phone: 08001974150

First published by AuthorHouse 2/26/2007

ISBN: 978-1-4259-6216-6 (sc)

Printed in the United States of America
Bloomington, Indiana

This book is printed on acid-free paper.

TO BEA

Who says war-time romances never last? For 62 years Beatrice Blau has given me a fabled life. More importantly, we have had a fabled life together. The secret – we fell in love and have never fallen out. Throughout the years, through joys and sorrows, sickness and health, births and deaths, victories and defeats, laughter and tears, ups and downs and overs and unders, we have had each other. I'm crazy about my wife and have been from the moment we came together. With all my heart, love and affection I dedicate this memoir (our memoir) to my beautiful wife Bea.

"To dream the impossible dream,

To fight the unbeatable foe,

To bear with unbearable sorrow

To run where the brave dare not go.

To right the unrightable wrong,

To love, pure and chaste, from afar,

To try, when your arms are too weary,

To reach the unreachable star!"

"Impossible Dream," Man of La Mancha

CONTENTS

PREFACE

While reading Jack Welch's biography, "Jack, Straight from the Gut," of his life and success at General Electric, I began thinking of all the stories of men and women who didn't achieve success with the help of the Corporate Ladder but who did it by themselves. They did it by dedication, hard work and an unwillingness to let failure deter them. At times they borrowed money from family and friends and always paid it back. They built warm, friendly relationships with their employees and customers. They used courage and ingenuity to create opportunities. All this gave them enormous satisfaction knowing they started with very little and wound up with a business that enabled them to provide their families with a very satisfactory quality of life.

Reading Jack Welch's manner of running GE, his employee relationships, developing management, making investment decisions, etc., I found myself thinking, "Hell, he didn't invent anything new. Most of us in small business have done these same things every day of our lives. It's just the dollars are different."

While big business runs the world, certainly in the United States, it's small businesses that are the real heroes in seeking and many times achieving "The American Dream."

I've written my own story, starting with nothing but desire. Fifty-five years of dedication, hard work, heartbreak, luck, tenacity, courage and fierce determination to succeed, it is the same story of millions of small businessmen and women in the United States. Each one could tell his or her own story and they all contain one similarity. They started with little or nothing and succeeded. For those readers who may wonder whether they themselves can do it, I hope this book will encourage them to try. It can be a wonderful life experience.

To those of you who have tried and are trying, I dedicate this small book. Who says you can't dream and achieve the "Impossible Dream?"

GROWING UP IN THE DEPRESSION

We are talking about 1927, the Depression. Every family in our neighborhood and the families of all my friends were having trouble making ends meet. These were very hard times. Very early I wanted to earn my own money. Aside from the fact it was helpful to our household cash condition if I didn't have to ask for money from my parents, I just wanted to earn my own money.

Around the age of 10 I began working in the public parks on weekends and holidays. This meant pulling a wagon selling popcorn, crackerjacks, candy and Coca-Cola. I learned to sing out my wares using the upper part of my mouth and nose, getting good sound and not hurting my throat. It is about Coca-Cola that I make my first confessional. I'm alerting my readers, you will hear more confessionals in the course of this narrative. It occurred to me if I took two bottles of coke and one bottle of water, carefully opening the coke, mixing all together, I would have three bottles

1

of coke. The sale of the third bottle was all mine. Little did I realize I had invented diet coke!

Because I was an energetic worker I was occasionally given preferred assignments. Rather than having to pull a wagon, I was put in charge of an open booth selling Vernons Ginger Ale. This ginger ale was issued in paper cups from a dispenser. The number of sales was determined by the number of unused cups remaining at the end of the day. I couldn't resist. As people bought and drank their Vernons they would usually throw the paper cup away. I would then recoup the best looking ones and serve them to other customers. I'm embarrassed to admit, sometimes the cups were soggy from use, but the customers didn't seem to mind. I, of course, was ecstatic. Instead of making 50 cents for my long day's work, I would occasionally make up to 75 cents.

Why did I start looking for the edge, or at times cheating if I didn't get caught? It started with the difficulty we kids had trying to make some badly needed money. While it's not a justifiable rationalization, I was among kids who were doing almost anything to make some money. These were depression years. We were not concerned with morality. We did not feel we were in any way engaging in criminal activity, just what we kids were doing. In fairness to my parents, they had no idea what we were doing. They were totally involved in trying to survive and keep our small family afloat.

My father, a slender man of 5'9", was in the restaurant chinaware business. He purchased his products in

Southern Ohio, the capital of pottery manufacturing in the U.S. He trucked his purchases to his store just off downtown Cleveland. My older brothers, Harold and Sanford and I spent many hours lifting, stacking and unwrapping chinaware. In our house we always used seconds – dishes that had been cracked or broken. To this day I can't go into a restaurant without picking up the chinaware to see by whom it was manufactured. We still have a few of the chipped and cracked dishes among our family heirlooms. Pa was a hard worker. I like to think he helped shape my attitude towards work.

I started loving baseball while still in elementary school. My immigrant mother took me to my first ball game when I was 8 years old. The game meant nothing to her, but she knew I loved baseball. It was in Cleveland's League Park (now gone) where, on a misty afternoon, Tris Speaker made one of his famous "shoe string" catches. He raced for the ball, did something like the splits and caught the ball on his forward toe as he slid on the ground. I was hooked.

The Cleveland Indians distributed bleacher seat tickets to all the schools in Cleveland. While in elementary school, when the time came near for the distribution, I was especially nice to the girls. I sort of liked the girls and still do, but my real motive was to ask for their tickets, which they generously gave me. Collecting about 15 to 20 tickets, I would travel to a neighboring school and trade for their game, usually game for game, or two St. Louis Browns games for one Yankee or Philadelphia game.

When the season started I hitchhiked, or for ten cents, rode the streetcar to League Park. There I met up with hustling kids from other city-wide schools and commenced trading. With luck and energy I went to 15 to 20 different games during summer vacation, sat in the bleachers and lived for double-headers. Nothing in my Depression experience equalled seeing a ball game at League Park.

In Junior High (middle school) I was the only kid who asked and received permission to leave school in time for opening day. Games started at 3:00 p.m., long before night baseball.

It was at a baseball game that I learned my first valuable lesson in business. At the end of a game, kids were allowed onto the field and would race to the player who had caught the last ball, usually an outfielder or 1st baseman, who gave the ball to the kid who got to him first. About 10 feet from home plate a box was imbedded in the ground where baseballs were kept for the umpires. At one game I worked my way down to the fence so I could race onto the field at the end of the game. While everyone ran out to the outfielder after the final out, I ran to the box. When I opened it, I was rich! I stacked several balls on my arm when I looked up to see a huge umpire peering down at me. I slowly let the balls fall and I was no longer rich. But I learned a valuable lesson I've carried with me through life. Had I taken one ball and ran before the ump got there, I would have that ball today. The lesson: *at times it's better to take a small profit.*

I've always felt one could learn something helpful from every work experience. Through those years I worked in the public parks, at football stadiums, selling ice cream bars outside the Cleveland Municipal Stadium, selling ice cream at the National Air Races, selling fruit off a street wagon, even soliciting for a siding salesman.

In my junior year in high school I got a Saturday job selling shoes in a low-priced ladies shoe store in downtown Cleveland. While the product was worth the price, the job requirement was that every customer who came into the store had to go out with a purchased pair of shoes no matter what. A customer was "turned over" to another salesman or supervisor 3 or 4 times, if necessary, and usually a sale was made. I can still remember our supervisor who intimidated us all and who seemingly never lost a sale. I heard he went on to Rabbinical school and became a Rabbi.

While a senior in high school I purchased a morning paper route for $20.00 and a bike that went with it for $6.00. I always wanted a bike. It was my first bike. The job meant I got up each morning at 4:00AM, rode my bike in the dark to pick up my papers, The Cleveland Plain Dealer, folded the papers and proceeded into the streets adjoining Kinsman Avenue to make deliveries. I had 50 to 60 customers. After completing the route, I returned home at 6:00AM, had several pieces of toast and hot chocolate, slept for a half hour and got to school at 8:00AM. Did I mind the schedule? Not at all. I loved it, especially the nap. On Saturdays I retraced my route to collect from my customers.

I had a successful senior year, played on my school football and tennis teams, wrote for the school paper and participated in other school activities. Whenever possible, I took a nap. At the end of the year I sold the route, including the bike, to another eager beaver. I had earned and saved $235.00, which was my tuition to college.

UNIVERSITY OF MICHIGAN

I applied and was accepted for admission to the universities of Wisconsin and Michigan. To this day I feel good I selected Michigan. Wisconsin is a great school and I'm sure I would have had a good college experience there. But Michigan I love to this day.

It didn't start out that way. The summer of 1936 I hitchhiked to Ann Arbor to line up three jobs. I worked in a restaurant for meals, worked for the National Youth Administration (NYA), a program of the New Deal to assist college students at 25 cents an hour and sold shoes on Saturday at Klein's department store in downtown Ann Arbor. After my first Saturday at Klein's, the manager offered me a regular job each afternoon and Saturday with a guarantee of $6.00 per week. It meant giving up the restaurant job.

Most of my high school friends in Cleveland went to schools in Ohio, especially Ohio State. Our family situation had deteriorated. My mother and father had separated. I was depressed and wanted to get away by myself and start my life all over so I went to Michigan. I wish I could say my Freshman year was a great time but it wasn't. Aside from being lonely, I was overwhelmed by the academic requirements despite an honor roll career in high school.

Because of my work schedule I made few friends, attended practically no school activities, not even Saturday Big Ten Football games and at times felt real sorry for myself. At one time I was so depressed I thought of quitting but was disuaded by my older brother Harold.

In my Freshman year everyone went home for Christmas Holiday. I continued to work at Klein's Department Store until 10:00PM Christmas Eve. With two suitcases full of unread books, I hitchhiked to Cleveland, 180 miles away, in a snow storm. I arrived home the morning of Christmas Day. It will come as no surprise to readers who also took books home on vacations to make up neglected work, I never once opened a book. By the time I graduated from Michigan four years later, I never bothered to take a book home during vacations.

Prior to the Easter holiday, the manager of Klein's asked me to work the entire Easter week. Getting up my courage, I agreed only on condition of a guarantee of $25 for the week, an unheard of demand. I knew I could earn that amount for Klein's. I could sell shoes. It was fun listening to him complain and grouse and finally accept my offer. It was a confidence building moment. I worked very hard giving Klein's a very profitable week, and more than covered my guarantee. That was it for me at Klein's. It was spring, Ann Arbor was beautiful, I was "rich." I left Klein's to become a full-time student, including going out for and making the Freshman Tennis team.

Shortly after returning home from my Freshman year my father died of Coronary Thrombosis, a young man of 53. How many times I wished I had come to know him better, that I had spent more time with him, that he had waited a few more years when his condition would have become treatable and curable. He was a hard-working man with a commitment to provide for his family. He left me with that legacy.

Between his death and recognizing my first year at school was not successful, I decided to stay home, get a job and go to night school, planning to return to Michigan a year later.

It was back to selling ladies shoes. An ad for a Saturday salesmen at the Cleveland May Company brought me to the women's shoe department. That turned into one of the most helpful experiences in my young working life. As I said, I could sell shoes and very soon my ability and conscientiousness came to the attention of a man who, in my memory, is my quiet hero. He was Floyd Page, a highly literate, elegant man, manager of the department. I had already been promoted to a regular weekly job selling shoes in the low price section of the department. The best job was selling high priced shoes, usually done by the most experienced and oldest salesmen. After a few months, to my complete surprise, I was moved forward to the high priced preferred section, causing a certain amount of antipathy among my fellow salesmen and sales women. My station was close to Mr. Page's office.

Floyd Page liked me. He would call me into his office during a slow work day to talk. He was very political and I was a political novice. He was a strong Republican who disliked the Roosevelt Administration and particularly hated Madam Francis Perkins, the first woman Secretary of Labor. He couldn't stop berating her. It was my first election. I enthusiastically voted for Franklin Delano Roosevelt and was totally caught up in the optimism of the New Deal.

Cleveland College was located across the Public Square from the May Company. I enrolled in night classes taking American Literature and French. Mr. Page asked me to stay on at the May Company promising me increased opportunities, but I was determined to go back to school which he understood. After I went back to Michigan, Mr. Page sent me train fare to come back for May Company Sales days and made sure I was compensated the maximum pay scale. In return, I gave him and the May Company my best effort and everyone was a winner. I regret to say, after I graduated, I didn't keep up my relationship with Mr. Page. He meant so much to me during those years. I've since made it a practice to remember as much as possible to stay in touch with people I've met on the way who helped and influenced my life.

I returned to Ann Arbor in the fall of 1938. Once again, it was an NYA job and a job at a diner restaurant close to the campus. The general rule for working in a restaurant was one hour of work for one meal. My job was to peel a sack of potatoes that usually took one hour. Before long I was finishing in less than an hour, closer to 30 minutes. The owner of the restaurant got miffed and upgraded me to a dishwasher where I would work a full hour and he himself peeled the potatoes. Many years later I learned that a few years before me, President Gerald Ford had worked in the same diner. By sheer coincidence we were once on a flight to Nice with then ex-president Ford and his wife, Betty. I couldn't resist introducing myself and telling him of our common experience while going to Michigan. It was a most gracious and pleasant conversation about what it was like going to Michigan in the 30's.

My NYA job was cleaning rat cages at the Laboratory of Vertebrae Genetics. At the end of my Sophomore year I responded to a notice that the Hillel Foundation was participating in the annual United Jewish Appeal campaign. Hillel was and is a facility on college campuses enabling Jewish students to maintain Jewish relationships, practice religious rituals, emphasize the Jewish contribution to campus and public life and be a friendly hospitable hangout for lonely students away from home.

I proceeded to the Hillel House and volunteered to help in the fund raising campaign. This campaign was focused on bringing refugee German-Jewish students to the US, victims of Hitler's Germany, providing for their housing and subsistence and enabling them to continue their college educations. I was given 35 cards with names to solicit. I proceeded to collect contributions ranging from 50 cents to $5.00 from 32 out of the 35 and then asked for more cards. Unheard of. I was given more cards but equally important, the student director, Ronald Freedman and Hillel director, Dr. Isaac Rabinowitz, learned of my efforts. In my junior year, I was invited to live at the Hillel Foundation, an event that changed my life.

It was now 1939-1940. I had no more worries about paying for a room. I worked for meals as a waiter in a fraternity house, I continued my NYA job and everything began to improve, including my grades. My jobs at Hillel were to manage the library and edit the Hillel newspaper.

I learned a boyhood friend, Howard Metzenbaum, later to become U.S. Senator Howard Metzenbaum, a student at Ohio State, was selling chrysanthemums outside the Ohio State Stadium in Columbus, Ohio. Why not, I reasoned? I wanted to sell chrysanthemums inside the Michigan Stadium. After inquiring of the University of Michigan Athletic department, I learned the concessions at the Michigan Stadium were run by the legendary Jacobs brothers, one of whom became the manager of Max Schmeling, one time world heavyweight champion. One rainy night I hitchhiked into Detroit to the Olympic Arena where Sammy Slaughter was fighting. After the fight I managed to find the Jacobs brother representative. He was a very nice man. I told him what I had in mind and assured him chrysanthemums would not be in competition with his products. Because he wanted to help me, we entered into an agreement – 40% to the Jacobs brothers on the gross sales price of each flower.

Having the chrysanthemum concession at the Michigan stadium was the beginning. First I had to find the flowers somewhere in Detroit. After 2 or 3 mishaps with wholesalers, I located a grower who grew beautiful flowers, would cut them for me early Saturday morning at a price of $3.00 a dozen, 25 cents each. Next I had to arrange for distribution. I lined up my classmate friends to cover all the entry gates to the stadium, reserving the most important gate for myself. I also figured out a way to get these salesmen into the game after I sold their student tickets for them. I was on a roll. The game was at 1:00PM. At 11:00AM our price for a chrysanthemum was $1.50 each which held until about 12:30PM. As we got closer to game time the price would drop, rarely less than $1.00. A colorful chrysanthemum on a cold Autumn day in Ann Arbor at a football game was a real show of affection and a relatively easy sell.

I learned much from selling chrysanthemums at the Michigan Stadium, an activity I continued for 3 years, including the football season of 1941-1942 after my graduation. When it came time to pay my salesmen (classmates), they "had to drop their prices early" and everyone's gross was different. But what the hell. They had a good day and so did I, usually earning between $35-$50, a fortune in the late 30's.

Not everything went smoothly. When Michigan played Minnesota one awful wintry day, very few people showed up and I had about 30 dozen white chrysanthemums unsold. Desperate, I hit upon the idea of housing them in a meat market freezer. The following week Michigan played Ohio State and white was part of Ohio State's colors. I retrieved the flowers and managed to sell them albeit at a slightly discounted price. To my horror, the flowers had no staying power. I doubt if any of the flowers were left on the stem after the first quarter. I must confess I made myself scarce that day, more or less hiding up in the stands. That too was a lesson. Don't panic. Try to figure out a way to limit your losses, but still take your losses.

To this day I think back on those great Saturday afternoons, sitting in the stands warming my hands in my pockets full of money, mostly coins, from the sale of those chrysanthemums, watching Tom Harmon, Forest Evashevski and those wonderful Michigan teams of 1937-1941.

Years later, at my 40-year reunion, sitting with legendary Tom Harmon, I told him what I did while he played football and that I always regarded him as my silent partner. He brought the people to the games and I sold them chrysanthemums. Always a man of dignity and class, Tom did not ask for a share of the profits.

Summer vacations from Michigan meant finding a job to earn much needed college money. After my sophomore year I was lucky to get a job as a playground director in the Cleveland Public Parks. Who could have predicted 43 years later, I would become the President of the Los Angeles Recreation and Parks Commission? More about that later in this memoir.

The following summer, out of about 500 young men applying for a job at Thistledown Race Track, miraculously I was chosen. My job was to take entry tickets. We were paid $3.00 a day. Occasionally I ran wagers for people in the stands. Best of all, I soaked up the excitement and love of horseracing.

In my senior year, to my total surprise, I was appointed Student Director of Hillel, a prestigious appointment that included an annual salary. Ronald Freedman, who was instrumental in the appointment of me as Student Director, went on to the University of Chicago to earn his Ph.D. He later returned to Ann Arbor and enjoyed a fabled career as a popular sociology professor. Ron founded the University of Michigan Population Institute and attained worldwide recognition in the field of population. Well into his 80s Ron, with his beautiful singing voice, served his temple as Cantor for the Jewish High Holy Days. We remain lifetime friends.

The newly appointed Rabbi at Hillel was Juhudah Cohen from Los Angeles. Despite our age difference, we became very good friends. He filled my head with the glories of California and as this document will record, he was right.

I feel fortunate to have chosen the University of Michigan. My senior year was the happiest and most successful time at Michigan. With the earnings of the football season and the salary from Hillel, I could focus full-time on my school work. Being Student Director helped me develop skills in communication, public speaking, diplomacy and that great catchall – how to get along with all kinds of people.

I graduated on June 21, 1941. The next day, June 22nd, the German Army marched into the Soviet Union and it was clear to me we were heading into the war. President Roosevelt, recognizing the role air power would play in the event of war, established a massive program to train 50,000 civilian pilots in a program called Civilian Pilot Training Corps (CPT). I had always been a reader of dime pulp novels about American, British and German Flying Aces during WWI and early on I was an enthusiast of flying. The National Air Races were held in Cleveland and I can still recall the pilots and types of planes that thrilled me and the thousands of fans who attended. I saw pilots Roscoe Turner, Lowell Bayles, Jimmy Doolittle and Charles Lindberg among others. I immediately enrolled in the Civilian Pilot Training Program.

WORLD WAR II

My base for Civilian Pilot Training was the Cleveland Municipal Airport. I still recall the first time my instructor told me to take the joy stick in the Piper Cub on my initial flight with the following instructions, "Don't hold it like it's your cock and you're about to jerk off." I liked flying at once and found myself very comfortable in flight. I received my pilot's license and graduated to the advanced course in Aerobatics which I loved. I enlisted in the Navy Air Corps.

While awaiting my call-up, I decided to build myself up physically and took a job as an ice man for the Cleveland Ice and Fuel Co. The steel ice tongs weighed 15 lbs and it seemed that everyone who bought ice for ice boxes, before refrigerators, lived on the3rd, 4th or 5th floor. The blocks of ice were usually 25 or 50 pounds. While a pretty good athlete, I never had much upper body strength and had a hell of a time carrying the ice. I was quickly demoted to delivering 100-pound sacks of chopped ice to restaurants. For me, it was a no-win wrestling match to put the sack on my shoulder let alone deliver it to the restaurant or bar. This time I was demoted to the ice house. Here large blocks of ice, 200 pounds or more, were manufactured and sent down a shoot to be cut into smaller sizes. My job was to keep the blocks sliding in the shoot or they would stick and not move. Prying them loose required the help of the foreman who, I was sure, had a brain frozen by his years in the ice house. I dreaded having a block stick, but those damn things seemed to have minds of their own and did stick regularly to the hostile consternation of my foreman. Not only didn't I build up my body, quite the contrary, I was fired. En route to becoming a Navy pilot in World War II, this was the one and only job from which I was ever fired.

We started pre-flight training at the University of Iowa. I loved pre-flight. I was twenty-three years old, felt great physically and was nuts about sports. In the morning we attended classroom sessions in recognition, navigation, physics and math. The balance of our day was spent swimming, running, hand-to-hand, obstacle course, marching, soccer, boxing, wrestling and calisthenics.

We swam for hours with our clothes on. We learned to take off our trousers in the water and make a life preserver of them. All swimming was with our head above water in the event we went down at sea. It was heartbreaking to see one of my classmates almost drown trying to fulfill his swimming requirement. He didn't know how to swim but wanted so badly to be a pilot. Regrettably, he didn't make it.

Several Big Ten football players were officers at Iowa pre-flight and we were able to watch some great Big Ten games.

Iowa Pre-Flight
Eager to go. Not a worry in the world.

While at pre-flight in Iowa I had two buddies whose names elude me. We spent hours side by side in marches and runs. It is painful to report one was killed training in fighter planes at Pensacola and the other died in another training accident. One of my buddies from Indiana had the middle finger on his right hand amputated to qualify for naval aviation. He used to kid he'd amputate his whole hand if he could now get out. He went on to become a terrific pilot.

Following pre-flight I was assigned to primary training in Pasco, Washington. This was the middle of the winter of 1942. We trained in open cockpit Stearman trainers. On more than one occasion cadets would return with faces badly frozen from the intense cold, especially ears that would freeze like full-grown cauliflowers. At Pasco we trained in advanced aerobatics.

It was then on to Corpus Christi, Texas which, along with Pensacola, Florida, was the final training base for aspiring Navy pilots. It was exciting and demanding. The flight training I received in the Civilian Pilot Training Program was extremely helpful all through my Navy Air Corps career. Thousands of U.S. pilots, then fighting the war, had flown their first planes in President Roosevelt's advanced-thinking Civilian Pilot Training Program. We graduated July 21, 1943. I applied for Navy bombers, but was assigned to a utility squadron stationed at Ford Island, Pearl Harbor.

After I met Bea, I was smitten

Enroute to Pearl Harbor, my first assignment, we had a 4-week stay at Naval Air Station, San Diego, while awaiting shipment to Pearl Harbor. I immediately came to Los Angeles where in a few days, with the help of Rabbi Cohen's sister-in-law, I met Beatrice Blau. I was thunderstruck. Never having been close to the wonderful feeling called love, I knew at once this encounter was different. She was beautiful, smart as hell, had a great build, a sense of humor and seemed to be interested in me. To support the war effort, Bea had interrupted her university education to take a job at Douglas Aircraft in Santa Monica. We spent three idyllic weeks together. I then left for Ford Island.

Ford Island, Pearl Harbor: Wonderful Hawaii

Hawaii was paradise. It still is. The beautiful Polynesian people, the glorious weather, the ever-changing colorful terrain, and the extraordinary sunsets had this boy from Cleveland Ohio in full-time awe. I loved the flying, my fellow pilots, I was young and raring to go. Besides, I was in love, completely smitten by Bea, optimistic about the war and our future.

I spent four months on Ford Island, during which time we flew to Midway, the place of the famous first victory over the Japanese Air Force and Navy Fleet after Pearl Harbor. To this day, I cannot comprehend the thinking of the Japanese rulers who believed they could invade, occupy, dominate and control the Pacific Islands thousands of miles from Japan. It boggles the mind.

Still fresh from the United States, I flew co-pilot on a rescue mission off of Hawaii to locate a pilot who had bailed out and was lost at sea for 15 hours. We were flying a Grumman seaplane with two engines mounted on top of the wing. The mission fanned out over 150 degrees. Flying at 500 feet above the water, my pilot miraculously spotted the pilot in the water. In order not to lose sight of him I dropped our yellow life raft as a marker. Circling the raft a few times, mercifully we spotted him again. We landed in a heavy sea, taxied over to him and I pulled him into the plane.

Taking off in a heavy sea became a problem. As we pushed power forward, the powerful waves stopped the propellers and prevented take-off. I then held the wheel full back while my pilot went to full throttle. After a dozen hard bumps on violent waves, one large bump enabled us to gain enough height to regain flying speed and flight. We dropped the pilot off at a medical facility on the uninhabited island of Kauai. For this seemingly rare achievement my pilot was awarded the Air Medal and I received a letter of commendation. Vacationing on now-developed Kauai years later I found myself regretting my failure to buy land after dropping off the pilot. I realized why I didn't. I didn't have any money.

I was then sent to Funafuti, an atoll south of Hawaii and Johnson Atoll along with three other pilots and crew. Our assignment was to maintain and fly Gruman TBF torpedo bombers. I also flew to American Samoa for a short tour in SBD Douglas dive bombers.

Glorious Funa Futi Pilots and crew members

We rejoined our squadron on Tarawa in the Marshall Islands, the site of one of the bloodiest, costliest U.S. island invasions of the Pacific War. Flying B-26s, TBFs and the Gruman "Goose," a single engine seaplane, we did duty on the Marshall and Gilbert Islands, including Kwajelein, Majuro, Eniwetok, Tarawa and Makin. These are now part of Micronesia. Our primary activity was preparing the fleet for invasions, including towing targets, radar calibrations, photography, rescue missions and other assorted assignments.

After thirteen months, I returned to California. Bea and I married and are still happily married 62 years later. I was stationed at Moffett Field in Sunnyvale, California. After three months, I applied for a transfer to Navy bombers. I was sent to Hutchinson, Kansas for training in the Navy version of the Boeing B-24, the Navy PB4Y2, for the anticipated invasion of Japan.

A wartime romance lasting 62 years? Impossible!

While riding in a jeep to our airfield in Hutchinson, the word came that a huge bomb had exploded in Hiroshima, Japan. I don't think any of us knew the location of Hiroshima, or the magnitude of the destruction, but to a man, we were hysterically happy. The war was going to end and we had survived. Six days later the war ended.

UNIVERSITY OF CALIFORNIA - BERKELEY

Our first daughter Leni was born in Los Angeles. I was given early discharge papers and returned to Los Angeles. We decided to move to Berkeley where I would go to the University of California to work on a masters degree in economics. The only housing we could afford was in Richmond, 15 miles from Berkeley. The housing project was built during the war to house shipyard workers in the Richmond Shipyards. Our apartment was small, minimal, but we were young, in love and new parents of a delicious little girl. I was able to return to college thanks to the thoughtful G.I. Bill of Rights enacted by President Roosevelt. The G.I. Bill provided returning vets with tuition to attend universities of their choice.

UC Berkeley was and is a great university. It was loaded with ex-service men and women, extraordinary faculty, a beautiful campus and, of course, it was just across the bay from glorious San Francisco.

Irving Zeiger

I was interested in concentrating on labor economics. One evening I attended a union meeting of the United Oil Workers in Richmond. I met some of the workers. I also met C. Masterson who was soon to become a judge and George Miller, Jr., later to become an assemblyman and state senator. I was asked to head a statewide petition campaign in Contra Costa County, Proposition 16, to place a Fair Employment Practice Act on the California ballot that would prohibit discrimination in employment for race or religion. It was an exciting campaign and one in which I believed. Harry Bridges, whom I met, was the legendary leader of the International Longshoreman and Warehouseman Union. He was the Northern California Chairman. I offered to fly a plane and drop leaflets throughout the Bay Area supporting the petition drive, but wisely Bridges thought I was crazy.

We were asked to get 2,000 petition signatures. I asked Earl Robinson, composer of "Free and Equal Blues," "The House I Live In," and "Joe Hill" to open the campaign, to which he graciously agreed. We developed an enthusiastic hard working campaign and collected over 12,000 signatures to the amazement of everyone, including Harry Bridges. Proposition 16 made it on to the ballot, but was defeated in the general election.

I was then asked to head a joint labor committee of AFL, CIO and Railroad Brotherhood in support of the campaign of George Miller, Jr. in his first political effort to become a California Assemblyman. George was elected, served several terms, became a State Senator, ran for Lieutenant Governor in the losing Gubernatorial campaign of James Roosevelt versus Earl Warren and remained in the California State Senate for the balance of his life. The bridge connecting Richmond to San Rafael is the George Miller Bridge, named in his honor for his service to the state of California. Perhaps an even greater legacy of which he would be proud is his son, U.S. Congressman George Miller of Contra Costa County.

Meanwhile, I was working on my master's thesis, "Labor Organizer in California Agriculture." My research was enhanced by my ability to find and interview some of the original organizers of the "Factories in the Fields" of the 1930s.

The summer of 1947 I took a job in a Richmond Cannery, Felice & Perrelli. The CIO was challenging the AFL Teamsters union, the union in all the Northern California canneries. It was to be the largest union election since the General Motors election in 1940. I was a conscientious cannery worker, but my main activity was to convince fellow workers to vote for the Food, Tobacco and Agricultural workers FTA-CIO. We won our plant, but the AF of L won the overall election. Impressed by my organizing efforts, the National Office of FTA-CIO offered me a job as a National Organizer but I declined in order to continue at Berkeley.

To earn badly needed money, I worked for the Research Division of the International Longshoreman and Warehouseman's Union analyzing labor contracts, an activity that served me well in later years. From there I became organizer and business agent for the United Public Workers CIO, a small struggling union.

I recall a memorable moment in my union organizing career. Among our members were the nurses and hospital attendants in the newly established Kaiser Permanente hospital in Oakland, California. Dr. Sidney Garfield had convinced Edgar Kaiser to establish a hospital for the workers in the neighboring Richmond Shipyard who were building hundreds of Kaiser cargo ships during World War II. The American Medical Association hated what Edgar Kaiser and Dr. Garfield were doing to the point of kicking Dr. Garfield out of the American Medical Association for promoting "socialized medicine." Today, Kaiser Permanente is the largest, most respected and successful provider of medical services to families throughout America.

But back to the story. On one hot summer afternoon I was in a meeting with Dr. Garfield where I kept pounding on him to increase wages and benefits for his nurses and hospital attendants. Dr. Garfield stopped me in my tracks with the following: "Listen, Irving, if you think you can run this hospital better than I can, here," whereupon he reached into his pocket and presented me with a key ring of about 50 keys for every room in the hospital. "Here," he said, "You do it. I'm exhausted and want to go to Hawaii for a badly needed rest." Of course I never took the keys, but it was one of the better moments in my union organizing career. I occasionally tell my friends had I taken those keys, I might now be the head of Kaiser Permanente hospitals. Our daughter Susan was born in the Kaiser hospital in Oakland. Bea and I remained members of Kaiser Permanente for many years. When I started my first company with employees, I immediately enrolled and paid for them and their families in Kaiser Permanente.

Organizing government workers was extremely difficult and at times impossible. It is ironic, in later years United Public Workers merged into the Federal, State, County and Municipal Workers, today one of the largest growing unions in the United States.

We returned to Los Angeles in 1949. With the arrival of David, our third child, I couldn't do justice to my family with the demanding hours and meager pay as a union organizer. I left the trade union movement.

STARTING TO
BUST MY ASS

I really never thought of myself as doing anything other than being in the business world. My father spent his life in it, I was in and out of business throughout my early years and I felt confident I could make a living for my now growing family. I never aspired to "being rich". I was a depression child. Surviving and providing comfort and security for my family were my goals.

During the war my brother Sanford had migrated from Cleveland to Los Angeles. He was unable to serve in World War II because of a serious skin problem. After working in a machine shop during the war, he and a working friend, Spencer Wright, started a business by purchasing aircraft hardware products that were being released by the War Assets Administration.

The War Assets Administration (WAA) was formed to sell off excess materials bought by the government during WW II. Millions of tons and millions of dollars worth of new, unused products of every type were auctioned on a daily basis. When the history of this activity of the War Assets Administration is written, we will find that many of today's great corporations got their start by being successful bidders at these auctions. Equally, the availability of unused excellent materials enabled thousands of companies to begin producing new products of all types stimulating the economy of the postwar period. War Assets' products needed by the aircraft industry were instrumental in enabling manufacturers to proceed with the development of advanced military and commercial aircraft. Sanford Aircraft, Sanford and Spence's company, specialized in aircraft components and it was in this area I continued to buy and sell inventories throughout my business life, more about which we will read in this document.

Sanford and his partner were my first employers. They rented a large quonset hut and I literally started from the bottom. Chuck, Spence's brother, developed a device that could separate aluminum from steel. I went to North American Aviation and Douglas Aircraft where I purchased barrels of floor sweeping from their surplus yard. Using Chuck's device, a magnetic roller that held the steel and dropped off the aluminum, we would then sell both items as scrap, getting a better price for the aluminum. Occasionally there were good, saleable components that had dropped to the floor at the aircraft plants. We also got jobs salvaging material. On several nights my wife Bea came to the quonset hut to help me in the salvage work. In a short time it became clear this was not a way to make a living.

My brother Sanford suggested I take a desk in his sales department and try to broker parts on my own, i.e. finding what buyers needed and then locating their requirements with a small profit to myself. Not having anything to sell I didn't do very well. Finally, he suggested I come to work for Sanford Aircraft in the Sales Department and I came running.

Being the kid brother of the owner was an awkward position for me. I worried the other salesmen thought I would be treated with favoritism. I wanted none of that and was determined to help the company by doing as good a job as possible. I quietly set a goal for myself to earn $500 for the company before morning coffee break. After a month or so I was meeting that goal, to the surprise of Sanford and the annoyance of the entire sales force.

When I first reported for work I had no list of possible customers to call. I asked the accounting department for the names of companies that had been customers but who were no longer doing business with Sanford Aircraft. I began calling on these former customers and within a short time I was able to bring many of them back. I loved the work. Whatever free time I had I spent in the warehouse and inspection department familiarizing myself with the products I was selling.

Sanford Aircraft was a growing successful aircraft parts distributor. My brother Sanford had a great personality. He was tall, handsome, bright, funny and one of the most promising young men in the new industry. At age 34 he was struck down with a brain tumor of unknown origin. He was operated on by Dr.

Tracy Putnam, a world renowned brain surgeon, but to no avail. No one could explain it. It was a family and personal tragedy that has never left me.

Sanford had been in New York and had purchased a huge inventory of aircraft components located in six warehouses in Brooklyn. The price was $200,000 for 1,000 tons of material. I told Spence, Sanford's partner, I could no longer work at Sanford Aircraft. I couldn't handle the intense heartbreaking pain. He asked me if I would consider going to New York to organize Sanford's purchase and to integrate the material into Sanford Aircraft. Talking it over with Bea, we both felt it would help us deal with our grief and we accepted the offer.

I proceeded to Brooklyn. I lived in a hotel for three months while Bea stayed in Los Angeles to rent our house and then brought our three small children east. My first look at the inventories was exciting. My subsequent look made me realize the quality and quantity of the material was far less than Sanford had seen or was led to believe. I learned that an electronic dealer who put in very low bids on all war assets auctions accumulated this material, which clearly included many undesirables. He was probably the only bidder. That was possible because of the vast amount of material being released by the War Assets Administration.

I set to work transferring the material to one warehouse and began marketing as best I could. It was not long before I realized the mediocre quality of the products and the difficulty in sales proved it. I also began getting an education in meeting people who wanted to make "side deals" such as building inspectors willing to sign off on fire extinguishers and other safety requirements for a bottle of whiskey and other unseemly suggestions.

After six months of modest results we decided to try to find a buyer for the entire inventory. I contacted a very large scrap metal company in Baltimore. We had been told our inventory was 1,000 tons. The professionals from Baltimore showed me it was no more than 600 tons. In short, we had been taken. I was a little fearful of the owner who sold us the deal. He was a suave, niftily dressed man with long manicured finger nails. It was also rumored he was close to the Mafia.

Determined to salvage the situation I approached Tony, I believe that was his name, told him what I had learned about the declared weight of the inventory and what the probable real weight was – about 60% of 1,000 tons. I mildly suggested this could be cause for legal action. Tony, for reasons known only to him, agreed to a heavy discount providing he received the amount we owed him in cash. We paid off Tony. I had saved our company $70,000.

That interesting time working in a warehouse under the Brooklyn Bridge resulted in my meeting many ambitious up and coming young men who would go on to highly successful careers in the aircraft components industry both as distributors and as manufacturers. Lester Avnet, a bright literate young man founded Avnet Co., to this day one of the largest electronic distributors in the world. I fondly recall the day Lester phoned me and suggested we go into partnership. I declined, but it was a boost to my confidence. Lester Avnet used his new wealth in philanthropy, in the arts, in culture and in medical research in New York and Israel. He died in his 60's, a great loss to the electronic distribution industry, his family and the many causes to which he was devoted. Many of the people I met in Brooklyn remained friends and business associates in the years that followed. The Brooklyn warehouse of Sanford Aircraft was sold to David Weisz, a Los Angeles auctioneer. David asked me to stay on and sell material until the date of the auction, which I did.

It was Spring 1951. We had rented a beautiful house in Amityville from a young dentist who had been called away to the Korean War. The house was located on the Great South Bay of Long Island, complete with a small beach and boat dock. It was very helpful to Bea and me emotionally and worked wonders for our family. 1950 - 51 were among the great years for musicals on Broadway and we were able to attend many of them.

By the time the auction of the Brooklyn inventory took place I had sold off enough material to offset the total price David Weisz paid for the entire inventory. Following the auction, I received a $5,000 bonus for my good work with which I immediately bought a small motor boat, "The Mad Skipper." We spent the rest of the summer in Amityville enjoying the beauty of the Great South Bay where we water-skied, swam, fished and took in as much of New York City as we could manage.

After a few weeks I realized I had to figure out a way to earn some money. My first act was to have calling cards printed with the name of a company, "Liberty Aircraft Co." It sounded like a powerful name and a big active company. I had good knowledge of the location of aircraft hardware in the Los Angeles area and I called on potential customers hoping to broker material. On one occasion, I called on a customer with only my card – no pencil or paper to write down his requirements. I phoned him the next day with the items he needed and received a purchase order. In a short time I made enough sales brokering material to get us through the summer. We bought a new Kaiser automobile with the money we earned and saved and had a wonderful healthy summer. The time had come to head back to California. We took four weeks, stopping at Niagara Falls, Cleveland to see old friends, Mount Rushmore Memorial, Red Rock Canyon, Yellowstone National Park, Grand Canyon and Jackson Hole. Our now grown children still remember that exciting cross-country trip.

BUSTING MY ASS

Back home in Los Angeles I was now faced with reality. What to do to make a living? The surplus market, i.e. material from the War Assets Administration, was very active. There seemed to be material everywhere. I received requests from business friends from New York and the Midwest to locate products they needed. Auctions were held everywhere offering a variety of aircraft and electronic components. Working from my home I attended auctions, seeking out inventories and material and bidding on government offers. I became very active in buying and selling components. I was especially fortunate in that several men I met during my time in Brooklyn trusted me and gave me opportunities to procure material for them while earning a commission for myself. On more than one occasion I purchased products for them at the price they were willing to pay and sent it to them without any profit for myself. It is a policy I exercised throughout my career and it was rewarding.

My garage became my office and warehouse. I was the salesman, secretary, switchboard operator, warehouseman, shipping and billing clerk. It was exciting, challenging and even fun. There was a neighborhood covenant against running a business from your home. At times I had to do some fast talking to convince the neighbors in charge of enforcing the covenant that nothing was happening at our house, even though a huge Trans-Con truck line was delivering large boxes to my garage.

Always open to suggestions on how I might earn a living, I picked up on a comment made by my examining dentist: "If anyone could invent sugar-free chocolate he could make a fortune." Seizing on the comment and anxious to make a fortune, I immediately contacted a childhood classmate I grew up with in Cleveland, Eli Seifter.

Eli and his brother Sam were different from the rest of us. They had a chemistry set and lab in the cellar of their apartment building. Following World War II, Sam became a prominent research physician at the Albert Einstein School of Medicine in New York City. Eli was then working in the research department of Monsanto Chemical in St. Louis, Missouri. Eli, too, was anxious to make a fortune and proceeded to experiment to develop sugar-free chocolate. After several weeks of back and forth phone conversations, Eli sent his results in a shoe box. By the time it arrived the chocolate had turned white. The time had come to give it the authentic consumer test. David, now 5, seeing the contents of the shoe box, happily remarked, "Oh boy, chocolate!" He immediately spit out his first mouthful, making an awful sound. With that spit out went Eli's and my fantasy about making a fortune.

Eli Seifter went into the field of medical research developing several products and patents and never let his inability to produce sugar-free chocolate keep him from having a remarkable career.

I continued my interest in flying by subscribing to "Trade-A-Plane," a lively trade publication where I noticed a continuing demand for Venturi tubes which were no longer being manufactured. The Venturi tube, mounted on the wing of small aircraft, provided suction that operated Turn and Bank and Rate of Climb instruments. Subsequent development eliminated the need for Venturi tubes but thousands of small aircraft were still dependent upon them.

I arranged to have a Venturi tube machined. It was rather crude but seemed OK. Before I advertised Venturi tubes for sale I had to make sure they worked. I myself had been dependent upon the Venturi tube in my flying. I arranged to test the instrument at the Northrop Corporation wind tunnel. After the test Northrop asked me if I would like to buy the wind tunnel! Not completely satisfied, I located a bush pilot and attached the Venturi to the wing of his open cockpit plane. We flew out over the Pacific Ocean. The friendly pilot, sitting in the front seat, kept turning around to talk to me, resulting in our losing air speed. As a former pilot, I was sure we were going to wind

Irving Zeiger

up in the Pacific Ocean. I kept hollering at him to keep his air speed up. I had him make several maneuvers while testing the Venturi tube. It worked. I sure was relieved when we finally made it down safely.

Advertising in Trade-A-Plane, I was surprised and pleased at the number of orders we received. I had the tube swedged by a shop that made products for the meat packing industry. The base was die cast and mounted by welding. The fun part was putting on the label, which was done on our kitchen table, frequently by my mother-in-law. Over the years, when driving through California, coming upon small airports, our children would run over to the planes to see if our Venturis were mounted, as they were. For 8 years the Liberty Aircraft Venturi was a quiet source of income and a lot of fun. Today, Venturis have been replaced by advanced instrumentation.

My first banker was my mother-in-law. Too early in her marriage, her husband died of tuberculosis and she was left with four children. She managed to salvage his small insurance and, with the help of a friend, invested in small houses and an apartment. I learned much from her. We were good friends. My mother-in-law lent me $500 to $1,000 early in a month. I drove her to her Savings and Loan in downtown Los Angeles and if the money was returned to the bank before the end of the month she received interest for the full month. I always managed to repay the loan before the end of the month, drove her back to the Savings and Loan where she collected her interest. As my business began to improve, I relied less and less on my understanding mother-in-law, but I am forever grateful to her for helping me get started.

I purchased a small truck. My father, who always had a truck, used to say if you had a truck you could always make a living. He was right. For two years I made a nice living. I was home with my children, was able to go to their school events, played basketball in the yard with them and had fun. The few vacations we were able to take had us driving through California in a station wagon, stopping at motels with a swimming pool for the children while I called on potential customers. We all got to see and know much about fantastic California and I would occasionally make a sale to help pay for our vacation. Did we have great vacations? We sure did.

Nevertheless, I knew this wasn't what I wanted to do for the rest of my life. It wasn't an ego matter but somehow, being a graduate of the University of Michigan with a major in Economics, having had two years of graduate work in economics at UC-Berkeley, having been a Navy pilot with a good war record and an honorable discharge, I just had to find a career other than driving around in a Ford truck from auction to auction.

Among all the products I sold over the years - - hardware, hydraulics, electrical, instruments and electronics, I began to focus on electronics, particularly electrical connectors. I rented part of a warehouse in Inglewood, moved the material from my garage to Inglewood and began to focus seriously on getting into the electronic industry. For shelving I went to the North American Aviation surplus store and purchased huge boxes used to ship propellers. Each box was enormous and seemed to weigh a ton. Fortunately I had the help of Bill Inglis, a weight lifter from the University of Southern California. The two of us managed to transport them to the warehouse where they became my permanent efficient shelving for several years.

Bill Inglis went from warehouseman to become an outstanding popular salesman for our company. He later went on to a successful career and life as a creative realtor in the Los Angeles real estate explosion. It always felt good to me when my company provided the opportunity for young people to move on and pursue their own dreams.

Unexpectedly, I got a call from Dumont Aviation with an unusual offer. You may recall I had unhappy days and nights collecting scrap from aircraft plants and sorting it for usable material as well as saleable scrap. On one occasion Nat Dumont, owner of a leading aircraft hardware distributing company, Dumont Aviation, had asked me to sort out some mixed material he had bought. We did a poor job of sorting. Badly as I needed the money, I told Mr. Dumont to forget the invoice and offered to re-sort the material at no charge.

Like many others, Dumont Aviation got its start purchasing from the War Assets Administration. Nat Dumont purchased a large winery warehouse in Pomona, California to house his huge inventory of war assets material, which included all types of aircraft components. Dumont Aviation's interest was aircraft hardware. Nat called me and asked if I would like to take the electrical material on consignment. Did I ever! My only cost would be transportation and insurance. We agreed on a 50 – 50 split. I insisted on one understanding, i.e. there would be no second-guessing on sales prices. Nat knew I would get the best prices I could and he would get an honest count. Every two weeks I rented a large semi, drove 45 miles to the warehouse in Pomona, selected material, helped load the truck and drove back to Los Angeles with my heart in my mouth, having had no experience driving a huge loaded semi. Electrical products made available to me by Dumont Aviation were a huge assist in getting me started. For several years it was a mutually benefitical arrangement for both companies. On a few occasions, at my request, Nat financed the purchase of inventories I couldn't finance myself. In every case there was a quick profitable payoff for both of us. Nat Dumont and I remained good friends.

Nat Dumont was very successful, became a community benefactor, a generous contributor to UCLA, a close confidant of California Governor Pat Brown and was extremely well liked by everyone throughout his creative lifetime.

The leading aircraft electrical connector manufacturer in the U.S. at that time was Cannon Electric, located in Los Angeles. I wanted to become a distributor of Cannon connectors. I now learned one of the definitive business lessons of my life. I was told a sales person of a company I was dealing with was very friendly with the distribution department at Cannon and she would get me an introduction. I was very grateful and waited for the contact. I waited. I waited. There was always a reason she couldn't make the contact. I did what I have always done since. I picked up the phone, talked directly to the distributor sales manager, told him how qualified I was and that I wanted a Cannon distributorship, to which he responded, "Thanks for calling, we were looking for a distributor in your area". The lesson, never forgotten, is *go direct*. Don't depend on friends or relatives to get you there. Do it yourself. I've passed that precious information on to my children and have watched with pleasure how helpful that bit of advice has been to them.

Our First Promotion:
"We work around the clock to fill your order."
L-R: Beverly Dupre, Bill Inglis, Elsa Broastedt and Irv

Once we received the Cannon distributorship I couldn't wait to get to work. Much as I loved my family, now Bea, Leni, Susan and David, I could hardly wait for the weekend to end so that I could be back at work Monday morning. I would frequently spend two to three hours every Saturday morning at the office to plan, correct and order inventory and analyze opportunity. During the week I called on customers, on occasion parking the car and running from one prospect to another. I refused to pass up any address that might be a prospect.

It was customary to invite customers to lunch. Since I was still driving a beat-up second-hand Buick, I would borrow a newer car from one of my employees to make a better impression on my customer. It was fun. It was challenging and it enabled me to make friends I have to this day.

When we were young. L-R: Helen Venamen,
my first secretary; Bea, Irv, General Manager
Elsa Broastedt and Ed Wiseman

By 1958, Liberty Electronics (I had changed the name) was one of Cannon Electric's largest customers in the United States. When the company decided to have their connectors assembled by distributors, Liberty Electronics was the first distributor chosen to prove the effectiveness of the new program.

We had a large sales force and an outstanding inside order department. Our general manager was Elsa Broastedt, smart, congenial and the first woman General Manager in the electronic distributing industry. Our company had a wonderful group of employees. We offered a paid medical program for employees and their families long before medical programs became widespread.

Very early I concluded if you want to build a company you must rely on and *encourage your employees to make decisions.* Some employers have trouble letting go. Not I. Occasionally mistakes will be made, but overall, encouraging your key employees to make decisions will be the difference between growth and no growth. Elsa directed the inside sales department of Liberty Electronics and in a relatively short time we became Cannon's 5th largest customer in the United States.

Douglas Aircraft became our largest customer. It's a story worth telling. For many months I tried to call on Douglas buyers but my competitors had been there before me and I could never get by the receptionist. We lived in Westchester, a neighborhood bordering the Los Angeles Airport. I learned of the formation of an Indian Guide's father-son organization. My 8-year-old son David and I joined up. After several meetings an overnight trip was planned to which we went. To my amazement and amusement three of the Indian Guide fathers were employed in Douglas' purchasing department, 2 for the products we sold and one as the head purchasing agent. I had no trouble thereafter getting past the receptionist. Liberty Electronics became a major supplier to the new DC-9 and other Douglas planes. I remained friends with my Indian Guide fathers long afterward and followed the careers of their sons, now grown fellow Indians.

When I think of how people join country clubs to make contacts, invite buyers on cruises, golf tournaments, sporting events, you name it, and here it all happened because of the wonderful father-son activity, Indian Guides.

Because I've always been an aspiring jock, Liberty Electronics formed a softball team and entered the Inglewood Softball League, swift pitch, every Monday night. Most of our players were employees, husbands of employees and a few friends of employees. I was 35 years old and played second base. I was a fair fielder but better than average hitter. Monday night was important to me. My teammates were usually in their twenties. I continued playing for 16 years until I was 51 years old. The Inglewood Times printed the batting averages which I collected and are among my most cherished documents.

Selected as "Truest of the Blue" – Dodger Stadium

Just to see if I could still hit, on my 80th birthday an employee drove me to a batting cage where I still managed to hit a few in the 40 mph cage.

In order to augment the growth of Liberty Electronics and to avoid dependence upon connectors only, we became distributors for Bourns Trimpots and Microswitch. We formed Electro-Sonic Components to distribute electrical components and hired Edward Wiseman to run the company.

The new kid on the block was transistors. The transistor had just been developed at Westinghouse and the rush was on. A leading new transistor company was Transitron of Swamscott, Massachusetts. Practically every distributor in the country coveted this line and so did I. On a sales trip in the East I called on the Transitron distributor sales manager and after a lengthy discussion convinced him Liberty would be a good distributor and he agreed to appoint us. That was exciting.

A week after returning to Los Angeles, this same distributor sales manager called to tell me that Leo Bakalar, president of the company, didn't think our company was big enough to handle Transitron. Leo Bakalar, together with his younger brother, David, who was an engineer at Westinghouse when the transistor was invented, formed Transitron. In a short time it was one of the largest and most prestigious semiconductor manufacturers in the U.S.

After beseeching the distributor sales manager over the phone, I said I was coming back to see Mr. Bakalar personally. He said Bakalar would not see me. I was undeterred. For the first time I flew first class on the "red eye" to Boston. I wanted to be sure of a good night's sleep. My only suit, a dark blue, needed pressing. Upon arrival in Boston I rented a car, drove to Swamscott, found a dry cleaner, stood on the toilet while they pressed my suit and presented myself at

Transitron at 9:00 AM, only to be told Mr. Bakalar was unavailable. I said I would wait and I did. About 2:00 PM the secretary advised me it would be an hour, then another hour and another hour. I wouldn't quit.

At 5:30PM, with the plant closing down, Leo Bakalar came out. He was an elegant looking man, clearly in command. He invited me into a small conference room and proceeded to tell me why our company was not qualified to handle Transitron.

He then changed his tune and asked me about myself – a real switch. I told him some of what is in this document. I told him how I got into the electronics business by purchasing surplus electronics. His eyes lit up. He began to show interest, commending me for my ingenuity and energy. I learned later that's how Leo Bakalar made the fortune that enabled him, with his brother David, to launch Transitron. Bakalar was in shoe "findings", all the items that go into making shoes, acquiring his products in the surplus or open market not unlike the electronic surplus industry.

He made me commit to a hard financial agreement regarding purchases and timely payments including an advance of $50,000 before any purchases were made. This took a lot of scrambling on my part but I was able to borrow the money from the bank and we had the very desirable Transitron line. In a short time we became Transitron's largest distributor in the United States. Leo Bakalar and I became good friends. His daughter stayed with us when she came to Los Angeles where we hosted her to the motion picture studios and other Hollywood sites. I was invited to David Bakalar's wedding. Leo and his wife hosted our family, which now included three teenagers, in their home in Swanscott for dinner and a Louis Armstrong concert.

My first attorney was my brother-in-law, Louis Blau. Louie was a rising attorney in the entertainment industry. Following receiving the Transitron franchise, I came up with a marketing campaign: "Tex – we dominate the west in transitors." Very shortly thereafter, I received a letter from Texas Instruments, the world's leading manufacturer of semi-conductors, advising us we were invading their trade name and we should cease and desist.

"Not me," I said, and sent the letter to my brother-in-law, the lawyer. He promptly told me to cease and desist. "Why?" I said, "I love the idea!" "Because," my brother-in-law said, *"They pay their lawyer."* I ceased and desisted.

Just as everything was going great, I was awakened on a Friday night to be told our plant was on fire. By the time I arrived, the fire was out but the warehouse and the inventory were in a state of ruin. It was determined that the negligent handling of oil rags may have caused the fire. I sat up all night together with my warehouse foreman to make sure there would be no looting. The next morning, Saturday, many of our employees, hearing of the fire, came to the plant and began putting things back in place. I was OK personally until I saw, floating in the water, a drawing my 9-year old daughter had given me which I had posted in my office. I burst into tears.

Days of anguish and uncertainty followed. The phone company put in temporary lines and we were back in business on Monday morning. I was worried sick my insurance couldn't possibly cover the loss. I had kept good records and felt I could establish the monetary loss when the insurance company representative "advised" me to use a very competent insurance fire adjuster. While I almost recovered the value of the lost inventory, I suffered substantial loss in business not covered by insurance. We dug in, worked very hard and in a matter of months we were back to normal.

"Normal" also found me continuously short of money to finance the growing business, particularly the need to regularly purchase large amounts of semiconductors from Transitron. Battling to keep myself from being overdrawn at the bank, I engaged in the well-used technique of "kiting". Calculating when the creditor would cash the check and the bank transaction was completed, I would mail checks to Swamscutt, Massachusetts on Thursdays, figuring receipt there on Monday, deposit on Tuesday and have almost a week to cover the amount at my bank.

My bank was City National Bank of Beverly Hills, a new aggressive business bank, founded in a breakaway from the older established Union bank. Hugo Brink, (what a great name for a banker), a wonderful man, was my banker. He was generally responsive to my requests and whenever we completed a transaction, he would seal it with, "Thanks, pal, for the business". There was and always will be only one Hugo Brink.

On more than one occasion my timing on the kiting was faulty and Hugo would call to tell me I was overdrawn. I would then precede to suggest he "lose my overdrawn check," "hide it in his desk drawer," "drop it on the floor," and give me a few more days to make it good. Anything to buy time, to which Hugo would tell me he couldn't accommodate any of my wild suggestions because U.S. bank examiners were in the bank and wouldn't permit it. On one desperate occasion involving a very large check, Hugo kept telling me he couldn't help me because bank examiners were in the bank and wouldn't permit his doing what I asked him to do. Reaching for the moon, I said, "Hugo, how come every time I call your bank, the bank examiners are there? At the Union Bank, your competitor, they don't have bank examiners." Replied Hugo, "You move your account to the Union Bank, pal, and they will have bank examiners there!"

In the thick of the struggle

Even though Liberty had twelve outside salesmen, I didn't remain in the office but continued to call on customers. Aside from being a pretty good salesman, I wanted to be current with what was going on in the field. I learned early *the way to manage is not by command but by example and leadership.*

It was at this time I experienced a bitter lesson in discipline. I was in pursuit of a Tantalum capacitor distributorship, a much sought after franchise. I dealt with the local representative who had stated I would be given the line. In my enthusiasm, I began advising customers we would soon have Tantalum capacitors. A bright ambition buyer at Lear Aviation, Tony Hamilton, overhead me. A few weeks later I learned Tony had found an investor with $50,000, had gone to the Tantalum factory in the South with the check and wound up with what was to have been my distributorship.

Tony went on to build a highly successful electronic distributing company, merging with Avnet Electronics and dominating the industry for more than a decade. One way or another, Tony was destined to be successful, but my open mouth enthusiasm got him started. The lesson, of course, is *control your enthusiasm until you have closed the deal.* Or put another way, don't talk about anything you are working on to anyone before it happens. I confess, I still have trouble controlling my enthusiasm.

By 1958, Liberty Electronics was an exciting, growing company when a series of setbacks occurred. We always felt we were a better than average employer with wages and conditions far better than those in companies our size or even larger. None the less, one summer morning a union agent of the International Longshoreman and Warehouseman's Union (ILWU-CIO) confronted me with a dozen or so signed cards of our employees demanding a union. The cards did not represent a majority of the workers, some of whom were on vacation. My previous union experience gave me a good knowledge of labor law. I told the union agent I didn't object to a union, but I felt it was important that a majority of our workers be in agreement. I asked that recognition be withheld until our vacations were over and we could have a vote from all employees, a matter of a three week delay. Aside from all else, it was my legal right under the National Labor Relations Act. Ironically, it was the warehouse division of the ILWU which demanded recognition, the very same union I had worked for while going to UC-Berkeley. Foolishly, as events developed, the Union refused to wait, set up picket signs and called a strike. The majority of our employees continued to work and while it created some dislocation, the strike and union effort evaporated. No company employee who had supported the union lost his or her job. Not because it would have violated the National Labor Relations Act, but because it would have been unthinkable.

One moment in the strike is worth recounting. As a way of having the children of our employees know what their parents did, during the summer vacation we invited every child of each employee to work for one week, doing simple non-important minor tasks to keep them occupied. The wage scale for elementary school was 25 cents per hour, Jr. High was 50 cents and High School was $1.00 per hour. During the strike the union went to the Wage and Hour division and accused us of paying wages below the minimum. I was then required to raise all the children's wages to minimum wages, which I did even though their parents objected to the order. So much for being a nice guy.

The worst was yet to come. In the ordinary course of a working day, I received a phone call from Cannon Electric advising me our distributorship was being taken from us. The reason was we shipped a connector to North American Aviation that was crudely modified with surplus components. While our use of surplus was vastly reduced, we still continued to supplement our purchases from Cannon Electric in areas where their manufacturing was unable to keep up with the demand. This practice, while not approved by Cannon and other connector manufacturers, was quietly tolerated in the interest of their distributors expanding the sales of their authorized products. The connector we had shipped to North American was wrong and unacceptable. From the very beginning, perfect quality was our commitment. Our stationary contained an airplane in flight with the words "For Security in Flight". As a former Navy pilot I had a visceral feeling that had never left me of depending upon the perfection and integrity of the plane I was piloting or in which I was flying. Perfection in the products I sold for aircraft was and is my lifelong commitment.

I never saw the connector that went to North American Aviation. Caught up in the management and marketing of Liberty Electronics, I was not as attentive to quality control as I should have been.

Cannon Electric represented more than 50% of our business. We had 60 employees. I was desperate to try and save the company. I was advised North American Aviation would no longer buy from us and would damage Cannon's ability to continue to be a supplier. Unlike the practice of major company officials who blame lower echelon employees for violations, crime, bribery, fraud, you name it, I took full responsibility for what we had shipped.

I went directly to Bob Cannon, President of Cannon Electric. We were quite friendly. Liberty had been a terrific asset to Cannon. Again, taking full responsibility, I asked Bob for a way to prevent this disaster. He then advised if NAA would be willing to take us back as a supplier, Cannon would cancel the dismissal. I then went to NAA. In a cold austere office, I met with a NAA vice president and a lawyer. I bared my soul, took full responsibility advised them of the corrective actions we had put in place, my conversation with Bob Cannon and our very good record as a supplier to North American Aviation over several years. To no avail.

In succeeding years many large American corporations have misled the government, falsified test reports, screwed the government, shipped defective equipment, overcharged the government etc., yet continued to receive gigantic contracts, while a little guy like Liberty Electronics, after years of reliable, outstanding performance to North American Aviation, was about to be destroyed by an unfortunate shipment of a component which had never been on a piece of equipment or caused any trouble.

Exhausted, in despair, worried for my employees and family, I contacted Cannon and was assured Liberty could keep the Cannon line but only under new ownership.

I then contacted Wyle Laboratories, a quality control research facility which had become a public corporation. With no experience in these matters, in a panic and with limited assistance, I agreed to sell Liberty and Electro-Sonic Components for Wyle stock at $36.00 a share for a total of $1-million in stock. Wyle represented its annual earnings together with those of Liberty would be the basis for a secondary offering, enabling me to receive cash for my stock. Kept out of the sale was my inventory of surplus connectors. I was very unhappy with the sale. It broke my heart. The surplus connectors were my insurance. As soon as the sale was completed Wyle's annual earnings were revealed. Liberty's earnings from the sale represented the bulk of Wyle's earnings and Wyle's earnings alone were miniscule. It was clear to me I had been lied to and had been taken. I immediately filed a lawsuit demanding recission and restoration.

The lawyer I was advised to use, Meyer Raskin, was not a corporate lawyer but a divorce lawyer – my first mistake. I was miserable and dependent on others for legal advice. That, too, was another lesson. *Never make a decision when you are emotionally upset or depressed.* Take some time off. Regroup. Feel better. Then face the problem. The chances are you will make a better decision.

With no secondary stock offering from Wyle, I was without income. My insurance was a big inventory of excellent surplus connectors. Paul Jacks had been our warehouse foreman. I suggested we become partners and start a new connector company with the surplus inventory. Paul was a younger man, a committed bachelor who had come to us from working in a scrap metal yard. With guidance, he became a competent warehouseman. Paul balked at first, thinking he had a better opportunity elsewhere, but I talked him into joining up with me.

In a few days, Ed Wiseman, the hardworking young man who had been sales manager for Electro-Sonic Components came to me and said he didn't want to work for the new owners and asked if he could join up with me and Paul. I then did what was unheard of. Even though I provided the entire inventory and the money to start the company, I offered Ed and Paul equal partnership with myself, i.e., a three-way partnership.

My reasoning was these younger men would continue to work longer than I and the company would supplement our family income in later years, assuming there would be income from the Wyle sale. Little did I know then this company, to be called Spacecraft Components, would be the strength behind all my future endeavors. I was in my mid-forties and starting all over again.

We were broke but we weren't poor. Bea had gone back to UCLA, majored in Education and graduated Phi Beta Kappa. She took her first teaching assignment in Aliso Village Housing Project, a ghetto area in downtown Los Angeles. Very little of her modest teacher's salary made it home. Bea used it to supplement needed school supplies and lunches for the students.

We postponed David's Bar Mitzvah. He didn't mind at all. I had borrowed $1,500 from a friend and there was no way we would have a party while owing money to a friend. Three months later, the loan repaid, David's Bar Mitzvah party took place combined with Leni's high school graduation celebration.

TRYING TO GET
RICH QUICK

My business life came crashing down on me with the panicked sale of Liberty Electronics. I was consumed for months by the torment of second-guessing myself. It was a painful time in my life, but I was sustained by a wonderful wife, three exciting children and a loyal Springer Spaniel. I refused to go down for the count and instead set off on a course of trying to recapture my losses and reinvent my career overnight, a huge mistake.

Just prior to the sale of Liberty Electronics I decided to become a manufacturer of precision gears as there wasn't a precision gear manufacturer on the west coast. "Perfect Gear" stayed with me after the sale of Liberty Electronics. I kept it going for two exhausting years and finally sold it at a loss.

A former employee introduced me to an engineer who claimed he could refurbish giant vacuum tubes and give them new life, a good idea and much needed at the time. I set up a company, advertised our capability, received enthusiastic interest and orders, but was never able to deliver one refurbished vacuum tube. My engineer turned out to be totally unreliable and unstable.

My accountant, anxious to help, put me in touch with a bright electronic engineer who had a new concept for manufacturing printed circuit boards that would eliminate hand-mounting of components. The engineer was associated with a machine shop and I was given a one-year option to explore the idea. *I refused to recognize the invention of the computer chip.* After a year of hard work using my previous relationship in the electronic industry, I was able to interest a major manufacturer of resistors to develop and manufacture this new concept. My lawyer, Jack Schwartzman, came back east with me to negotiate the contract which called for a $100,000 investment by the resistor manufacturer and 25% of the sales price of the product to us thereafter – an unheard of deal.

When I advised the machine shop of the proposal, they did the unthinkable. Believing they were sitting on a gold mine, they advised me my option time had expired and they wanted a better deal. The manufacturer immediately terminated the negotiations, the machine shop got nothing and I was out of pocket several thousand dollars of expenses. I learned one thing: *never take an option with a time limit.*

Along came my advertising man who had come across a type of video equipment to be placed at check-stands in supermarkets, advertising store products. I personally carried that 40-pound piece of equipment to markets trying to develop interest only to learn after several months of hard effort that no one was interested in watching a film while shopping in a supermarket. Film is not a novelty. Shoppers know what they want and don't want to be distracted. The proceeds around the check-stands from candy, gum, cigarettes and magazines represent serious, profitable sales and the store owners don't want their customers distracted. For a few years following my efforts, very impressive film programs were tried in markets and they too disappeared.

The lesson to the above tales of failure is well worth remembering. *Stay with what you know. Don't think because you succeeded in one business you have the golden touch. The chances and odds are you don't have a golden touch. Most important, don't expect to achieve in a short period of time the success you achieved in your previous business over a long period of time. It won't happen. But again, stay with what you know.*

BACK TO ELECTRICAL CONNECTORS

So, after two unhappy years, it was back to electrical connectors for me. Liberty Electronics had been a leader in the distribution business. At our high point we had twelve outside salesmen. Now I began calling on customers all over again. I was Spacecraft Components sole outside salesman. I vowed I would never again be dependent upon a connector manufacturer for a distributorship as I had been with Cannon Electric. I felt then, as I feel now, Liberty Electronics deserved better treatment and support from Cannon based upon our years of outstanding service and our sales record of Cannon products.

Slowly, but surely, Spacecraft Components began growing. I will always be grateful to several former Liberty employees who identified sales opportunities for me. It was a tearful moment for me when I sold Liberty but I was rewarded by the relationships with my former employees that remained intact over many years .

My lawsuit against Wyle was at a standstill. It occurred to me that Frank Wyle, an arrogant man, never felt threatened because he assumed I was not in a financial position to pursue legal action against him. Financial inability to pursue their case has killed many small entrepreneurs who had strong legitimate lawsuits against larger adversaries.

Frank Wyle was wrong. He didn't know about Spacecraft Components and its growing financial strength. I kept urging my own attorney to proceed but nothing was happening. I then decided to see what the hell was the mystery that kept my case from going forward. Several afternoons a week I attended trials of cases that appeared similar to mine in the Los Angeles Superior Court. It was an education. *There was and is no black magic in law.*

Coincidentally, while riding up a ski lift in Sun Valley, Idaho, I shared a seat with a young lawyer from the nationally prestigious Joseph Ball law firm. I proceeded to tell him my trouble. He told me I was being mistreated ("screwed", I recall he said) and felt I had a case for the Bar Association.

I sought out the 5 best lawyers in the Los Angeles area and called them to set up interviews. I sure wanted Joe Ball. He had been on the Warren Commission of the J.FK Assassination but was too busy and offered one of his excellent partners. I declined. After two meetings with equally outstanding lawyers, I met with Herman Selvin of Loeb and Loeb, one of the oldest and most distinguished law firms in the West. Herman Selvin was at the top of his career, handling major cases in California and the United States.

Mr. Selvin, along with Howard Friedman, listened. He was empathetic but was handling a death sentence case in the California Supreme Court and didn't have the time. He strongly recommended his protégé, Howard Friedman. I, too, was impressed with Howard. They advised they could not go forward until I dismissed my present attorney.

I then called Meyer Raskin and told him because of his lack of attention to my case I was discharging him and wanted my $10,000 retainer refunded. He refused. I demanded he give me a time sheet of the hours and minutes he had spent on my case. Again he refused.

I then told him the names of the lawyers I had met with "all of whom would give you aces and spades" and all of whom had advised I was treated incompetently. I told him I was prepared to take him to the Bar Association. I reluctantly accepted $5,000 back and good riddance. I was later told I was the only client to whom Raskin had ever returned money.

Howard Friedman was and is a blessing. In a few days he became completely familiar with the case. I told him everything, the good and the bad. For him there were no surprises. *I believe a lawyer can only be as good as his client.* I was a good client – determined, honest and I had lost a good company I had built. I had treated people well. I had been lied to and cheated and I was anxious to go to trial.

During the sale to Wyle I relied on the financial representations of Wyle and their accounting firm, Arthur Anderson. The revelations of Wyle's dismal earnings caused a plunge in Wyle's stock, making the sale a disaster for me. I hired Segal and Wasserman, skilled accountants employed by companies following fires and disasters who needed help to salvage financial records. Joe Segal and Ted Wasserman were masters at unmasking questionable accounting. We demanded Wyle send his accounting records to his attorney's office where Joe, Ted and I spent many hours examining Wyle's books. After two weeks of intensive searching, we were certain I had been defrauded and passed our research on to Howard Friedman.

Wyle's company was saved by the Liberty acquisition and I was determined to be made whole. The opposing lawyers, Irell and Manella and Martin Gang of Gang, Tyre, Ramer & Brown, Inc. were from two of the most formidable and feared law firms in Los Angeles. Not to Howard who immediately began deposing them and pressing our case. To put it mildly, Howard overwhelmed them with facts, the law, and the merits of my case. After a month we were presented with an offer to settle, restoring a portion of my stock with cash. I was counseled by Loeb & Loeb to accept the offer but I declined. This is what I meant when I said, "A lawyer can only be as good as his client." I told Howard to tell the other side his client was "determined to go to trial, he couldn't talk to him, he was furious with the offer, etc. etc."

Within the week, Wyle increased the offer to approximately 85% of the original price. In spite of my anger and deep-seated feeling I had been cheated, I reluctantly submitted to the argument of the hazards of a trial, the costs, and the unpredictable outcome. I still get upset with myself when I think of the settlement. I was robbed by Wyle Laboratories.

Spacecraft Components continued to grow, becoming one of the major buyers of surplus inventories from OEM's, airlines and products released by the Government.

Throughout this memoir "surplus connectors" have been mentioned. Surplus connectors are new unused connectors in their original manufactured condition, usually in their original or government packaging and are excess to the needs of manufacturers and the government. The connectors enter the market place following the completion of a government contract with manufacturers – Boeing, McDonnell Douglas, Lockheed, Martin-Marrietta, etc. The remaining component inventories are offered by competitive bids to the public. The U.S. Army, Navy and Air Force periodically release excess inventories no longer needed by the services, again through competitive bids. Over the years our company continued to be a successful bidder for electrical connectors. Very early we also began purchasing additional connectors directly from original manufacturers.

As a result of these purchasing opportunities, Spacecraft Components could be very price competitive and could afford to maintain large inventories of stock providing our customers with immediate delivery and service. Spacecraft Components today maintains the largest connector inventory of all connector manufacturers in the world, resulting in a worldwide customer base that includes the U.S. government, worldwide airlines, major airline manufacturers and thousands of suppliers of products to the military, aircraft, aerospace, high speed transportation and to thousands of suppliers and manufacturers in the commercial electronic industry. Considering it all started by my picking up barrels of scrap metal and sorting it just to sell the aluminum scrap (see Chapter 5), I feel pretty good about how it all happened.

FLIGHT CONNECTOR

With my thirty years plus background in sales, I felt I wanted to get into manufacturing. We were approached by a former Cannon Electric Connector engineer who suggested we develop an advanced firewall connector. These firewall connectors are located in the engine section of commercial and military aircraft. They must be very rugged and capable of continuing to operate in an atmosphere of 2000 degrees F in the event of fire in the engine.

We proceeded to develop a firewall connector that was an improvement over the only existing firewalls historically manufactured by Cannon Electric. In a surprisingly short time we had a superior product. I then hit the road calling on United Airlines, American Airlines, TWA, Delta, Eastern and Pan Am, offering "Flight" firewall connectors, the new name for our manufacturing company.

I long ago concluded the U.S. airline industry is unmatched by any other industry in its commitment to perfection. In my experience, if one could bring an airline a better, safer, more reliable component for their airplane, the airline would want it regardless of cost. Our Flight connector was the beneficiary of that exemplary thinking. The superb safety record of airlines transporting millions of people world wide daily attests to this commitment to safety and perfection and accounts for the U.S. airline and aircraft manufacturing industries' extraordinary contribution to modern civilization.

The new Flight firewalls received favorable attention, particularly from United Airlines. Larry Heinrich, a senior engineer, began testing Flight firewalls in various areas of their planes requiring greater strength and reliability in difficult challenging environments. United Airlines, then the world's largest airline, decided to use Flight connectors on the new McDonnell Douglas DC-10, then in design and advised Douglas of its desire. United was McDonnell Douglas' major purchaser of 1 billion dollars of DC-10's. McDonnell Douglas, besides using their own engineering expertise, paid attention to the engineering developments and requests of their customers.

Larry Heinrich spent his entire career at United Airlines and exemplifies the best in U.S. commercial aviation. His life and career are dedicated to making United's planes the best and the safest in the world. Though now retired from United Airlines, Larry is still being called upon by several airlines for help and advice in problem situations.

At one point, Ralph Zimmerman, Chief Component Engineer at McDonnell Douglas, questioned me as to whether this billion dollar DC-10 program could be entrusted in part to our small company of 35 employees. A fair question. While I never had any doubt we could financially fulfill our responsibility to Douglas, I exercised my best effort to convince the Douglas company of my company and my personal ability to finance their selection of Flight Connectors. I regard convincing McDonald Douglas of Flight's capability of being a reliable responsible supplier on the DC-10 as one of the very best achievements of my business career. Ralph Zimmerman at then Douglas Aircraft, later McDonnell-Douglas Aircraft and now Boeing was the same dedicated engineer I found in all my travels to dozens of maintenance hangars worldwide.

So there we were, 35 hard-working people who had taken on Cannon Electric (remember them?) with their 15,000 employees and we had developed a better, more reliable product and won a major contract. For the first 50 DC-10's, Flight Connector was the exclusive supplier of firewalls in the DC-10 maintenance manuals. Cannon Electric caught up to us six months later.

With limited experience in manufacturing and anxious to make sales, it became clear to me we were not developing any profit. I asked my wife Bea to analyze our cost structure. Bea, then and even now, finds errors in bank statements. Following her very effective work over several weeks, we increased our prices based upon realistic costs. I then went to our major customers who were subcontractors on the DC-10. I explained our unrealistic pricing. To the amazement of my accountant and many others, these subcontractors agreed to our new pricing on existing and future orders. It was a defining decision for Flight Connector.

A wonderful moment for me occurred when I took a month's lease on the last billboard entering Los Angeles International Airport. With a huge photo of the new DC-10, the billboard read, "Thank you, McDonnell-Douglas, for using Flight FirewallConnectors on DC-10." I sent framed photos of the billboard to all appropriate McDonnell Douglas management. I was told by friends at Cannon the people at Cannon Electric went nuts.

RXCOUNT – TRYING TO RESCUE PHARMACISTS

In an effort to assist a distant relative of mine who had an idea for a prescription counting machine for pharmacies, we found ourselves with another new company, "RxCount". Relieving the pharmacist from hand-counting pills sounded like a revolutionary idea. I called a Time Magazine reporter to tell him about our revolutionary product. RxCount immediately made Time magazine. We received offers from people all over the world willing to invest in RxCount. We thought we were going to rescue American pharmacists by reducing the amount of tedious time they spent hand-counting pills and by giving them more time to spend with their customers. Little did we know they didn't want to be rescued.

Many pharmacists were terrified of RxCount. Counting pills by hand seemed to be their most important activity and we were confronted with pharmacist responses like, "Then what will I do?" Or, "I can count faster than the machine". or "It's not worth the cost to have RxCount," plus dozens of other reasons. McKesson-Robbins, the country's largest pharmaceutical distributor, enthusiastically became our national distributor. We started leasing the machines and very early discovered McKesson-Robbins salesmen were gun-shy about demonstrating RxCount and preferred to just continue taking orders for pharmaceutical products on the shelves.

We quickly learned the lease price was too low to warrant sending out machines for approval and changed our marketing to outright sales. Nothing really worked. So much for helping a distant relative. Fortunately the new generation of pharmacists appreciates the application of advanced technology in pharmacies. We believe those brave pharmacists who bought and used RxCount found it made their work day easier and more pleasurable.

RxCount did provide me with a memorable relationship. An elegant senior gentleman appeared out of nowhere and applied for a job as a salesman for RxCount. M.A. Nation was his name but he preferred to be called "Lefty." Lefty Nation had been an Admiral in the U.S. Navy during World War II. Lefty was the landing officer on the aircraft carrier "USS Hornet." Now retired after 50 years in the Navy, Lefty was bored. I was in awe of Lefty having myself been a Lt. Junior Grade in the Navy Air Corps and here was a Navy Admiral working for me.

All Lefty wanted to do was sell the RxCount pill counter. He loved driving his car to naval and army hospitals, drinking coffee from his thermos and staying in navy officer's quarters. Lefty suggested we upgrade RxCount, which we did, resulting in increased acceptance and sales.

Though retired, Lefty remained a complete Navy man. One evening, he called me and said: "Irving, I apologize for calling you after the sun has gone down over the yardarm. Tomorrow I'm flying to Washington with other members of my retired Navy flight officers organization to lobby for greater support and finances for the Navy Air Corps. My orders are as follows: Reveille at zero six hundred, muster at San Bernardino Airbase at zero ten hundred and wheels off at thirteen hundred." As I said, Lefty loved the Navy.

Lefty Nation did a perfectly wonderful job of convincing Navy and Army medical facilities they needed RxCount. The truth is he saved the company by his sales effort. I'll never forget Lefty.

After eight exasperating years we managed to sell the company at a very discounted price, grateful we were still with the product we knew – electrical connectors. Several lessons were learned. *Don't trust your own enthusiasm if investing money is involved.* Take your time, research the venture carefully, look at the downside and above all, know what kind of investment may be necessary and how many years it will take to realize a profit. Equally, *the role and cost of marketing a product is second only to the quality of the product.* Over a period of time with hard work it is possible to recoup your investment. *What one never recoups are the years it takes from your working life.* RxCount was a case in point.

Fortunately I was able to stay focused on Flight Connector but RxCount was a distraction that shouldn't have happened. I take full responsibility for the folly.

BACK TO CONNECTORS

Together with Larry Heinrich of United Airlines, Flight Connector developed and United Airlines patented a self-locking device which I named "Herculoc". With Herculoc, guy wires which hitherto had been needed to keep connectors together, were eliminated. Over the years variations of Herculoc have become standard throughout the Connector Industry. The Herculoc was a contribution our company developed of which I am proud.

To expand our sales I began calling on our customers world-wide. We also qualified our standard connectors with all Boeing Aircraft and the new Airbus in Toulouse, France. In anticipation of meeting with Air France and Airbus, I decided to improve my Freshman French. From my plant in Hawthorne, each noon hour, I bicycled to El Camino College three miles away and took a French course. With a bottle of "vin rouge" to the professor and an "A" on the final exam, I felt reasonably confident I could survive in France while extolling the advanced qualities of Flight Connector. The times I had to use my French I struggled but made myself more or less understood and overall helped Flight Connector. I did wind up a nervous wreck!

The years 1970 to 1980 were among the most challenging and interesting years I spent in the connector industry. We made a significant contribution to safety in flight and earned wide recognition for this achievement. I love the airline industry and personally enjoyed visiting with engineers, buyers, executives and visiting maintenance hangars of airlines worldwide. Building Flight Connector was the most exhilarating and hard-working time of my work life. We were manufacturing a firewall connector that was more reliable than existing firewall connectors. We were contributing to greater security in flight.

Running a small company of 50 employees and competing with connector giants was nerve-wracking and challenging. Our giant competitors didn't believe we could succeed. It was a day-to-day effort to convince customers Flight Connector was capable of supplying their connector requirements. I thrived on the challenge – strengthened by a small group of determined, dedicated engineers, machinists, operations managers and assemblers who were caught up in the excitement and were committed to our success.

So there we were, the principle supplier of firewall connectors on the new McDonnell Douglas DC-10, with 50 employees and not a lot of money. Creditors for past due bills assaulted me. I became very eloquent in convincing suppliers to give me more time in which to pay. They, too, needed money to pay their bills.

Union Bank of California refused to renew our loan of $100,000. The word of our financial straits had gotten to ITT Cannon Electric, our competitor, fed to them by a disgruntled discharged engineer. To compound the problem, we had a union which was pressing us for wages and conditions I considered unreasonable in the light of our fragile financial structure. I was spending most of my day trying to appease and cajole irate suppliers desperate to be paid.

Making Flight Connector a success – the biggest challenge of my career

Despite the concern of my wife Bea, I went to my friends, offering them 1% of stock in Flight Connector and 10% interest on a loan of $25,000. Bea and I personally guaranteed the loan. The bank interest rate at the time was 7%, so 10% was very attractive. In a short time I raised $275,000, paid off Union Bank and ended my 15-year relationship with them.

I then went to some of my large creditors with an audacious proposal. I offered to pay a large portion of their bill at once in exchange for forgiveness of the balance. There is nothing new about this method of dealing with debt and I was determined to try it. Flight Connector was fighting for time and money. I assured my suppliers we planned to stay with them as we grew and they, too, would benefit from the success of Flight Connector. I was thankful that many of my suppliers, including major corporations, responded to my appeal to take less on their bills. In return, we kept our word and as Flight Connector continued to grow, they remained our preferred suppliers and always got paid in full, mostly on time.

Manufacturing, unlike distributing, required a continual input of cash for tooling, machinery, engineering, testing and all sorts of unforeseen problems. Before long, we found ourselves still fighting the cash battle. I called a friend of mine, Seniel Ostrow, one of the co-founders of Manufacturer's Bank that was established by a number of successful businessmen in the real estate, scrap metal and garment industries. At my first meeting with the Manufacturer's Bank loan officer from whom I was trying to borrow $200,000, he commented, "That really isn't enough. You need at least $300,000." Unheard of from a loan officer! My experience to date was whatever amount I wanted to borrow, the loan officer reduced my number. Manufacturer's Bank lent me $300,000. I became a loyal customer of Manufacturer's Bank for many years. At their request I made radio commercials telling of my extraordinary experience with the loan officer and the entire bank. With the strong support of Manufacturer's Bank, Flight Connector was able to go forward.

My job, besides making believers of my employees, partners and customers, was to sell Flight Connectors worldwide. Together with my wife Bea, we traveled the world clocking thousands of flight miles and hundreds of flight hours. It was hard, even exasperating work, sometimes rewarding, sometimes not. I was undeterred. I met interesting, intelligent engineers and buyers from many countries. On occasions these visits resulted in new friendships, home visits and dinners with wives and families. Some of my experiences calling on European Airlines stay with me. One morning I flew from London to Sabena Airlines in Belgium where I had a meeting with engineers and buyers, then to KLH Royal Dutch Airlines in Amsterdam for lunch with engineers and buyers, then drove to The Hague to visit a customer and back to the airport, arriving back in London at 8:00 p.m. the same day.

On another occasion I left my hotel room on the left bank of Paris early in the morning, no coffee was available, got onto the Paris Peripherique in a pouring rain, tried and failed to find my customers at Le Bourget Airport. I then drove to Charles DeGaulle Airport which was under construction and the few signs standing were in French, retreated back to Le Bourget, stopping en route to go to the bathroom French style in a field, still raining, tracked down my customer for an unsuccessful meeting, back onto the Peripherique to Orley Airport for a meeting with engineers in which I demonstrated Flight Connector in my fractured French, then a one hour failed search around the airport for a customer and back onto the Peripherique at 6:30 at night, still in the pouring rain when I burst into tears from exhaustion. I had not had breakfast, lunch, or a between break. So much for the glamour of Paris.

On one occasion while vacationing in Florence, I planned on visiting the Paris Air Show, the most prestigious annual aviation event in Europe. Early in the morning I took a train to Milan, a plane to Paris and a cab to Le Bourget, the site of the show. After spending three hours viewing the exhibits, I realized there was nothing there to help Flight Connector. So it was a cab back to Paris from Le Bourget, a flight to Milan, a night train back to Florence where I arrived at 6:00 a.m., 24 hours after starting out.

One memorable event occurred as a result of my making a favorable impression on George Rengasamy, Director of Procurement for Singapore Airlines. George was also chairman of the Far Eastern Airline Purchasing Agents Association. Following my sales call visit with him, George and his wife Iris took us to an outdoor chili crab dinner at a popular tavern rarely visited by tourists. George invited me to participate in the oncoming Airline Purchasing Association meeting in Taiwan. There we were, Flight Connector with its 50 employees, participating with Boeing Aircraft, McDonnell Douglas, Lockheed, Thompson-Ramo-Wooldridge and a couple of other giants in the industry.

I was asked to make a presentation of Flight Connector. While I'm not sure how effective I was, I do remember my little talk got a lot of laughs.

In October 1974 our agent in Israel informed us of a requirement to establish a modern connector manufacturing capacity at the government plant in Bucharest, Romania. The requirement seemed a bit over our heads, but our engineers developed a proposal and I was confident we could do the job. Our proposal was slightly in excess of one million dollars. Concerned we would be engaging in a violation of the laws relating to trade with an Iron Curtain country, I flew to Washington DC to the Department of Commerce and received clearance. Upon arrival in Bucharest, I visited the plant that issued the Request For Quotation (RFQ). The connectors they were manufacturing were ancient. I presented our proposal and received an enthusiastic response. During the succeeding two days I spent time with engineers and executives, all of whom were ready to go forward with Flight Connector. In three days we all became good friends, had meals together, met families and happily bridged the Cold War.

My illusion was shattered upon my return to Los Angeles. I never heard another word from anyone I met from the Romanian Government Connector company. I pursued the project, tried to find out what happened, called the Romanian Consulate and the Romanian Embassy in Washington to no avail. To this day, I wonder what happened. Four years later, I read that ITT Cannon Electric had been awarded a contract for seven million dollars plus for the project we had quoted.

These were exciting, challenging and fun years and they contributed to the growth and success of Flight Connector. From 1970 to 1980, it was unlikely there was a commercial airline flying anywhere in the world that did not use Flight Connectors. I am very proud of that accomplishment.

MY LIFE AS A MOTION PICTURE PRODUCER

In Hollywood, there is a saying – "Everyone has two businesses, his own and show business." I must confess I suffered from that condition.

A friend of mine, Irwin Lieberman, a television writer who had changed his name to Lee Erwin to ride out the Hollywood blacklist, told me that an Australian novel, "Walkabout" by Vance Marshall, a well-known Australian author, was available. It read like it would make a good movie. Here was my chance to be in show business – even better, to be a film producer.

My attorney was the same Jack Schwartzman who earlier negotiated the aborted deal to build a new circuit board device. Jack was a bright, funny, aggressive and ambitious attorney who worked for my brother-in-law, Louis C. Blau, my first and only free attorney (See Chapter "Busting My Ass"). Jack proceeded to acquire the rights to "Walkabout." Vance Marshall had died and his estate was only interested in optioning the book. Having had that sad experience with options I said, "Nothing doing," and would only buy the property outright, which I did for $10,000.

Irwin and a colleague, Lee Leob, were to write the screenplay and I was to be the producer. Sure enough a screenplay was written. Now what? The story takes place in Australia and deals with three children, including an Aboriginal boy who was on his "walkabout," an Aboriginal rite of passage wherein young boys enter into manhood. This rite of passage takes on many forms among young men worldwide.

With one wonderful exception, Gregory Peck, I knew very few people in the movie industry. I came to know Gregory Peck when I joined him in a gallant project to offset the turmoil of the 1965 Watts Riots by forming a theatre project in the inner city of Los Angeles. I treasure those meetings and phone calls with Gregory Peck. Besides his creative community and national contributions, Peck was attempting to become a producer. I brought "Walkabout" to him at his modest office in Universal Studios. Said Peck, "Irv, I offered to perform in an Australian story I wanted to produce for no salary and was turned down. No one wants to make pictures about Australia. The studio says it's like making movies about Abraham Lincoln." That was 1969. From 1980 on Australia has produced some of the best movies of the late second half of the 20th century. So much for timing.

An Academy Award winning screen writer whom I knew read the book and advised me there was no movie to be made from "Walkabout." A nephew, who was a "reader" at Universal Studios, also advised me that there was no movie in "Walkabout." This nephew, now ex-nephew, is one of the most successful writer-producers in television.

Several months later attorney Jack Schwartzman called to say Nicholas Roeg, a talented British cameraman/director was in Los Angeles and was interested in "Walkabout." I met with Roeg who liked the book but wanted to write a different screenplay. This would take Lee Erwin and Lee Leob out of the project. I spoke with both men who had no problem releasing their interest for $10,000, which I paid. This project was getting serious.

Jack then interested a newly formed production company, National General Corporation, again made up of people who had made money in sports, real estate, banking, etc. but who now wanted to produce pictures. A deal was struck. National General put up $25,000 for Nick Roeg to go to the outback of Australia to cast and find locations and also to write a new screenplay.

Several weeks later I met up with Nick in London where I had gone on business and he gave me the new screenplay to read. My first reaction was negative. I had no credentials judging a screenplay but I was hopeful I was wrong. I also recognized the limitations I had with respect to the creative aspects of the film and there and then decided never to put money into anything over which I didn't have some control or constructive input. I was wrong on both accounts, especially on the subsequent saga of "Walkabout." I wasn't the only party that worried about the screenplay. National General decided it no longer wanted to produce the movie with Nick Roeg's screenplay.

For the next year I heard rumors different people were going to finance "Walkabout," the most exciting was the sensational Beatles. But nothing happened. Fortunately, being a producer was not a serious diversion from my work at Flight Connector, at which I continued to work and which continued to grow. I had abandoned wanting to become a producer and was only hopeful somehow or other "Walkabout" would be made. Nick Roeg and I became good friends, a rich reward for my fantasy about making motion pictures.

In 1990, Jack Schwartzman called to say a couple of "producers" had shown up who wanted to produce "Walkabout." One was an aggressive opportunistic lawyer and the other was his client who had made a small fortune in the garment industry in Philadelphia. Would I sell my interest? Happy with the thought that Nick would make his first picture and being sufficiently disenchanted with the whole project, the answer was "Sure." I received back my investment and a little more, plus a fantasy profit of 15% of the producer's profit. The other condition was that my son David, soon to enter the University of California Santa Cruz, would work on the picture to which Nick happily agreed.

UC-Santa Cruz refused to hold David's entry a year and he was unable to work on the film. Nick went to the Australian outback and made a beautiful film of "Walkabout." "Walkabout" was a British entry in the 1971 Cannes Film Festival. Bea and I were in Cannes to enjoy the experience. Even though it didn't win an award, Nicholas Roeg went on to a distinguished, successful directing career. I am listed in the credits of "Walkabout" as Associate.

"Walkabout" was sold to Twentieth Century Fox for $1,000,000. It was released the same week as Fox released Elizabeth Taylor and Richard Burton in "Cleopatra." "Walkabout" ran one week and closed.

Despite promises for an accounting from the garment manufacturer producer, I never received an accounting or a penny. Over the years, "Walkabout" acquired cult status and appears intermittently on television and in art houses nationwide and has a loyal following. My only continuing relationship to the film industry is Bea and I occasionally go to a 4:00 p.m. movie, pay the senior price, buy popcorn, share a soft drink and have a very good time.

BACK TO CONNECTORS AGAIN

The connector industry, like all component industry, is forever growing and changing for the better. New advanced connectors are being demanded by the government requiring large financial commitments. I was now 60 years old and began to wonder whether I wanted to commit to additional new connectors and the required financial burden. Spacecraft Components was doing well. ESC was active but not very profitable. The time had come to sell Flight Connector, this time to a buyer with cash. The hell with selling for stock.

When selling a company it's conventional to find a third party to represent the seller. I never liked that procedure. Remember, early in this document I talked about "going direct." I followed my own advice and began calling the heads of companies who might be interested. Flight was profitable, had a lock on good business, good personnel and a promising future. While we weren't a major volume connector manufacturer, we had carved out a very profitable niche in the airline industry and we were engineering ourselves into the newer firewall connectors desired for the Boeing 757, 767, new Airbuses and other aircraft. We began receiving offers which I deemed entirely unsatisfactory. Ed and Paul, my partners, wanting to get out of the financial obligations of Flight, were anxious to sell at a low price. Flight was an excellent company and there was no panic. This time there would be a good sale.

As I was lying in a hospital bed at UCLA Medical Center recovering from hip surgery, Peter Cowell from England called to talk about buying Flight Connector. Peter heard Flight Connector was for sale from a company president who had made me a low offer and who thought he would eventually acquire us and had told Peter. "What did I say about keeping your mouth shut until the deal was made?" Peter left the president's office, went to a pay phone and called us. These were the days of corporate acquisitions. Peter, who had worked for an American company, developed financing from a British commercial bank and began acquiring small companies. His company, Dubilier, grew rapidly and was now on the British Stock Exchange.

We began exchanging information. A few weeks later Peter came to Los Angeles and it was love at first sight. Peter was in his early 40s, handsome, funny, preferred cold beer, played good tennis and was thoroughly likable. From then on our negotiations took place at my Mulholland Tennis Club on the courts or in the swimming pool.

Flight was a perfect fit for Dubilier and Peter acknowledged it. It was to be a cash deal. My unhappy experience with the stock sale of Liberty Electronics to Wyle forever cured me from selling anything for stock. The price was more than three times the offer my partners were previously willing to accept. The deal included 2 tickets for 6 days at Center Court Wimbledon. How could I resist?

*Peter Cowell – How could
I not like this bright, charming Brit?*

The personal friends who had loaned me money years earlier for the purchase of their stock were happily surprised with the return of their $25,000 loan, plus an additional amount almost equal to their loan. To this day, a few of them ask me if I have another similar investment for them.

Peter and his lovely wife, Diana and their children became family friends – a memory we cherish. We spent many hours together in Los Angeles playing tennis at our club and on his court in Oxford, England. We had lunches together in London, went to the Theatre with Diana and saw US play England in the World Rugby Cup match at Twickenham. We hosted his daughter when she came to LA. In a rare coincidence, on a family vacation in London, we were able to attend this same daughter's wedding in Oxford.

The acquisition of Flight Connector was a huge boost to Dubilier stock and Peter benefited personally. When we visited him at the wedding, he had purchased an estate in Abingdon, Oxford, was playing serious golf and was very happy. It pains me to write a few years later Diana called to say Peter dropped dead on the golf course. I can't forget him.

LIFE OUTSIDE OF MY BUSINESS LIFE

I was ready for some time off from work. Because I was politically active in Los Angeles, Mayor Tom Bradley appointed me to the Los Angeles Recreation and Parks Commission where I served as president in 1983. I was also a member of the L.A. Coliseum Commission during the sensational 1984 Olympic Games held in the Coliseum.

This brings me to an important thesis in this document. *Don't make your business your entire life.* Notwithstanding the demands of my business, I always found time for school May Festivals, Halloween Parades, Parent-Teacher meetings and just about every special school event in which our children participated. Sometimes it was stressful to get away, but I usually managed.

There was a price for all this. My very exceptional wife Bea willingly postponed her plan to complete her college education and begin a career in order to be with our children in their early years. Once the children were all in school, Bea returned to complete her degree at UCLA. She continued to take additional graduate courses at UCLA and USC. We were both actively involved in local and national politics.

In 1984, Bea worked as an intern in Washington DC for then California Congressman John Burton. In 1990 at the age of 73, we both spent three months in Washington DC as legislative aides to my boyhood friend Senator Howard Metzenbaum of Ohio. Besides my playing first base on the Metzenbaum softball team, "The Metz," Bea and I initiated legislation on low cost housing that was voted into law. It was a memorable experience that gave us insight into the workings of the federal government. We worked in the office next to the Senator in the Russell Senate Office Building. Senator Metzenbaum acknowledged our effort on the Senate floor. We were made part of the Congressional Record of the 99th Congress, Second Session.

Howard Metzenbaum was and still is my hero. We both grew up in Cleveland during the Depression. We both came out of families struggling to survive. We both started working and hustling early. Howard worked and hustled his way through Ohio State University and Law school (see Chapter 2, University of Michigan - Chrysanthemums at Michigan stadium.) Because he believed government can be a positive force, Howard became the youngest legislator in the history of the Ohio Legislature. Always entrepreneurial as he battled his way through the Depression, Howard began leasing parking lots around Cleveland which, after several years, became "APCOA" Airport Parking Corporation of America.

He eventually sold APCOA and committed himself to government full time. He was elected to the U.S. Senate and served three terms. He authored the bulk of his legislation on behalf of working men and women of America. He was frequently called "The conscience of the Senate."

Because of my background and serious interest in aircraft, I was asked to help Senator Metzenbaum evaluate the projected new Air Force F18 fighter plane. With the kind help of an Air Force analyst, I prepared a useful report for Senator Metzenbaum. Bea helped prepare a study on the controversial North American Free Trade Agreement (NAFTA) legislation. It was thrilling to see her sitting behind Senators Metzenbaum, Ted Kennedy and Paul Wellstone, bathed in Kleig lights, at a televised hearing on NAFTA. These were very heady times for both of us. We were there in April, May and June when Washington DC is ablaze with cherry blossoms and breath-taking flowers, a magnificent time to be in the nation's capitol.

At age 77, because of the demanding work required of a Senator and against the wishes of his many friends urging him to seek a fourth term, Howard decided not to run. He said, "Irv, I don't want to be one of those aging Senators who falls asleep at hearings and in the Senate Chamber." Howard Metzenbaum is a living example of striving for and achieving the American Dream.

Years earlier, Bill McClellan, a neighbor, came to me one evening and asked how I felt about building a tennis club on a large open piece of land 3 minutes from our house in the Hollywood Hills. Wow! We were off and running. My responsibility on the founding Board of Directors was to recruit members which I did with enthusiasm. Two years later, the Mulholland Tennis Club opened, an absolute jewel in the Hollywood Hills. Today, 40 years later, the Mulholland Tennis Club is one of the most popular successful membership-owned family tennis clubs in all of Southern California. Tennis has been my sport all my life and the Mulholland Club was and still is my own private sandbox. Regrettably at the age of 88 my body can't handle the demands of tennis, but I still keep my locker with my racquet in it just in case.

In August 1986 I joined my daughter Leni and my grandson Jesse Potter on the Great Peace March for Nuclear Disarmament. The March of 600 people started in Los Angeles and headed across the country. We joined up in North Platte, Nebraska. After two hip surgeries, I managed to walk between 10 to 15 miles a day, sleep in a small tent, eat strange food, use a portable toilet with confidence and had an extraordinary experience. While in Cleveland for my 50th high school reunion, I wrote an account of the Great Peace March for the Cleveland Plain Dealer. Senator Metzenbaum had the article made part of the Congressional record of the 99th Congress second session.

Without a doubt one of the most satisfying efforts in which I was engaged was the Kennedy Center

Honors in Washington, D.C. I didn't know Pete Seeger personally, but having watched the Kennedy Center Honors ceremony for many years I felt Pete Seeger, America's leading folk singer, was deserving of the honor. Pete had been a victim of the blacklist. He continued being actively involved in changing the social injustices in America and he fiercely opposed the Vietnam War. Our children grew up listening to and singing Pete Seeger songs.

I began an intensive letter writing and phone campaign directed at the Artist's Committee of the Kennedy Center together with the producers of the ceremony who were responsible for selecting the honorees. While in Washington I learned that very few appointments are made on the basis of merit alone. Appointments are a consequence of vigorous campaigning for the job. I enlisted fellow folk singers, congressmen and senators we met while working for Senator Metzenbaum, musicians of all types, even the Pete Seeger fan who was Secretary of Education and like-minded liberal and progressive individuals who were true Pete Seeger fans. I started the campaign in 1992 to no avail, no luck in 1993. It happened in 1994 to the disbelief of many of my friends who said it wasn't possible. I was told of Pete's selection while recovering from heart surgery. Good news is helpful to people in the hospital.

Back at full strength, Bea and I attended the exciting events of the Kennedy Center weekend, including dinner in the Benjamin Franklin room of the Department of State and the memorable ceremony itself where Pete Seeger was honored with an introduction of his life's career by Garrison Keillor. The Washington Post had a full page picture of Pete calling him "America's Favorite Commie."

Kennedy Center Honors with Pete Seeger, 1994

Years earlier I had become friends with Benny Carter, the legendary alto saxophonist. Following success with Pete Seeger, I proceeded to campaign for Benny to be honored at the Kennedy Center and began contacting dozens of his great jazz musician friends to help, which they did enthusiastically. In 1995 Benny Carter received the Kennedy Center Honor. Besides having dinner again in the State Department Benjamin Franklin Room and attending the formal ceremony, we were guests at a White House reception at which we met President Bill Clinton and his wife Hillary. We had our photo taken with them, among our most treasured photos. We cherish our friendship with Benny which continued beyond his last 95th birthday.

Kennedy Center Honors – Benny Carter, his wife Hilma, Bea and I - 1995

Bea and I are very connected to the Venice Family Clinic, a nationally recognized medical facility in Venice, California. The clinic is open to individuals with no health insurance and in need of medical care. Now the nation's largest free clinic, it serves upwards of 21,000 patients annually and handles over 100,000 patient visits. The Venice Family Clinic is presently being called upon to serve more patients because of the difficulty Los Angeles County is having meeting its escalating medical needs.

One of Bea's greatest pleasures is returning to her middle school, "Foshay Learning Center," now K-12, where each year she donates scholarships to graduating girls en route to colleges and universities. Bea also donated the Beatrice Blau Zeiger Corner to the Foshay library, a computer center for the students.

We are financially responsive to community needs when called upon and are lifetime supporters of the Los Angeles Music Center, the Mark Taper Theatre, the new Walt Disney Hall, the Los Angeles Opera, the LA Philharmonic orchestra and several educational institutions and programs. As lifetime members and supporters of the American Civil Liberties Union, the ACLU remains our deepest commitment to the well-being of America and our civil liberties.

All these extra activities over the years have helped me keep my equilibrium, helped me know what is important, helped me in dealing with all kinds of people, and mostly confirmed my belief that being successful in business and making a good living is not the be all and end all of our lives. My good friend Seniel Ostrow, who has since died, a legendary philanthropist and benefactor to many Los Angeles community needs, lived by the saying, "In this world it's not what we take but what we give back that makes us rich."

ARENA FOOTBALL, OR "WHO DOESN'T WANT TO OWN A FOOTBALL TEAM?"

In my experience practically every successful entrepreneur with whom I've associated fantasized about using some of his hard-earned money to own a sports franchise. I'm convinced today's baseball, football and basketball owners would prefer owning their team to being president of the United States. If their team should happen to win the World Series, Super Bowl or NBA, these owners will, for sports fans, be held in higher esteem than the president. But that's just my opinion.

One of my less successful or satisfying adventures took place when my good friend Byron Lasky and I agreed to be part of a new sports enterprise, "Arena Football." As I said, everyone wants to own a football team, especially frustrated jocks. I was one of those jocks as was Byron.

Byron had recently sold a television station for a bundle of money and was interested in finding other investments. Also, of course, he was a huge football fan. Coincidentally we were both Michigan graduates. The Los Angeles "Cobras" was our team. We were both caught up in the excitement of owning a sports team, especially a football team.

Mike Hope, a bright, personable young attorney with strong sports enterprise credentials, was our general manager. Our coach was Ray Wilsey, former assistant coach of the Los Angeles Raiders. We went to all the games. We played in Madison Square Garden where over the years I had watched basketball and hockey. We provided housing for our out-of-town players all of whom were hoping Arena Football might get them into the NFL.

Our league had teams across the entire country: Providence "Steamrollers" owned by Bob Andreoli, one of the country's leading costume jewelry manufacturers; Chicago "Bruisers" owned by Richard O'Heir, head of the largest asbestos removal business in Chicago; Detroit "Drive" owned by Mike Illich, owner of Little Caesar's Pizza; Detroit "Red Wings" and later the "Detroit Tigers"; New York "Knights" owned by Russ Berrie, the largest gift distributor in the United States; Pittsburgh "Gladiators" owned by the Arena Football league of which we were all partners; Los Angeles "Cobras" owned by Byron Lasky, majority owner, and myself.

All of us were beside ourselves with enthusiasm for Arena Football. The only people who weren't enthusiastic were the fans. A modest contract with Fox TV was no help. The television audience was miniscule. Attendance, or lack of it, was painful. Trying about everything, we just couldn't make it happen.

It was also a not-to-be-repeated experience where a band of hard-nosed businessmen disregarded all their business experience and savvy because they were so enamored with their desire to own a football team. I recall one meeting in a luxurious New York office suite where these highly successful owners spent time tossing a football around with former All Pro Chicago linebacker Doug Buffone, oblivious to the terrible investment in which we were blindly participating.

Everyone lost his shirt in our one (1988) season. Five years later, long after all of us had enough, the promoters of Arena Football managed to enter into a contract with ESPN to broadcast games. Counting on America's thirst for more football, Arena Football began to find an audience. Shortly thereafter, following Kurt Warner of the St. Louis Rams who went from Arena Football to the big show, the National Football League became a major partner with Arena Football as a training camp for potential NFL quality players.

Painful as was the loss of my money, being a sports franchise owner was a "rush." As a business decision it had to be one of my worst. To my wife Bea's credit she predicted from the start what would happen. She was right. That's what she gets for marrying a jock. Fortunately, I did not neglect Flight Connector, which continued to grow.

I was cured. I no longer want to own a sports franchise. That didn't prevent me from buying a minority interest in the Palm Springs Angels, an "A" farm team of the then Anaheim Angels. Fortunately, the team was sold to a bunch of eager buyers in Rancho Cucamonga where it seems to be doing all right. I think I broke even with the sale and I got to keep my "Palm Springs Angels" jacket.

SPACECRAFT COMPONENTS

With the sale of Flight Connector, Paul Jacks, who had been managing Spacecraft Components, elated with his good fortune, lost interest in work and sales and profits began to decline. He was anxious to leave the business. Ed and I purchased his stock. At the age of 68, I took over managing Spacecraft Components. Ed concentrated on ESC, Inc., where we manufactured connector accessories.

Clay Campbell, whom I saw as a diamond in the rough, came out of the warehouse. His working experience was in warehousing. While his skills in managing employees needed improvement, Clay quickly acquired knowledge of the connector industry and developed into a competent effective general manager. He enthusiastically attended a course at UCLA to improve his management skills. Clay grew up in Nova Scotia and began skating and playing hockey at a very early age. He continued to play hockey, coached junior hockey and participated in the annual hockey tournament sponsored by George Schulz, "Peanuts" author, who invited senior hockey players worldwide to play on his personal rink in Northern California. Time playing in the George Schultz tournament was not deducted from Clay's vacation time. We were proud of Clay.

Led by Larry Cohen, we developed an effective inside and outside sales force of capable men and women. Larry was one of our best salesmen at Liberty Electronics and was now at Spacecraft Components. He was hard working, enthusiastic and funny. Customers liked Larry Cohen. I continued to call on customers myself. Our advertising and sales material was unique, imaginative and helpful to our customers.

Spacecraft Components "All Americans"

When it became necessary to improve our plating capability, I spent many months with Mike Timen, a remarkable and talented young man with plating experience. All our connectors required plating. We bought and Mike built a plating plant that gave us the needed plating capacity to meet the growth of Spacecraft Components and ESC.

At the proper time, I negotiated the sale of ESC, Inc. to a New York stock exchange corporation. It was never a profitable company, but a good, solid manufacturer of necessary connector components. We profited by the sale.

We were still purchasing excess inventories. I was able to complete a transaction that seemed impossible to my competitors. My long history of dealing with Israel Aircraft Industry enabled me to arrange for Israel Aircraft to consign to us over $1,000,000 in inventory. Two years later I was advised by a Vice President of Israel Aircraft that this consignment deal was the most successful they had ever placed.

The availability of excess inventories was beginning to diminish. I was fiercely opposed to being dependent upon a manufacturer for product based upon my experience with Cannon Electric. We began developing and manufacturing our own series of electrical connectors. With good quality and good service, within a few years Spacecraft Components Connectors (SPC) were engineered onto projects worldwide and contributed substantially to our growth. Ed Wiseman developed a spectacular website that brought us hundreds of worldwide hits weekly.

By the 1990s our sales had risen from $3,000,000 annually to almost $10,000,000. But by the late 1990s the connector industry saw a continuing decline as did the entire aircraft and aerospace industry. Our neighbor, McDonnell Douglas, was purchased by Boeing. Northrup was purchased by Hughes Aircraft. Nationwide purchasing of aircraft components was reduced substantially.

As the need for connectors diminished in the airline and aerospace industries, we developed and manufactured connectors for the emerging high speed transportation industry that was finally developing in the United States as it had in Canada, Europe and Japan.

Spacecraft Components had come a long way from supplying connectors from excess inventories, often called "surplus," to an internationally known and trusted manufacturer of quality connectors for airlines, aerospace and now the worldwide high speed transportation industry.

Driving to work, usually one hour plus, then the same ride home in horrendous Los Angeles traffic, I began to feel my age. Some of the fun of going to work was disappearing. I had rounded 80 and everything got harder to do. I began to understand why corporations have mandatory retirement ages. Most of them are 65 or even 70. Ridiculous, I say. In those years I was still at my best fighting weight. But 80 was a whole different thing. I finally cut back going to the plant to two days a week, but kept actively involved at home by phone, fax and my secretary, Sally Hamilton. The truth was my intense interest in the work began to wane.

Clay Campbell awarding me
"Employee of the Year – in abstentia."

The industry had changed dramatically and had gotten away from me. I was no longer able to keep up. With the growth of the computer and the internet, my skills at marketing were no longer needed. I enjoyed making the rounds to all the employees as a morale booster but that, too, wasn't sufficient. With the exception of being available to deal with financial matters I was not making a meaningful contribution to the company. We had a good, mature, committed workforce and a dedicated, talented and hard working General Manager, Craig Wiseman, Ed's oldest son. Craig, a personable hard-working young man, became very knowledgeable of electrical connectors. Equally important, Craig related well to the new generation of engineers and buyers who now populated the connector industry.

On occasion at the end of the day, Craig would come into my office to bring me up to date on how we were doing. I found myself telling Craig about the history of the company rather than offering anything meaningful to help the growth of Spacecraft Components. I just didn't like not being able to contribute helpful suggestions. The time had come. I sold my interest in the company to my partner, Ed Wiseman. I was surprised to find how difficult it was to go into "retirement." I dislike the word.

As I complete this book it has been three years since, at the age of 85, I drove away from Spacecraft Components for the last time. Reviewing my voluminous files from the past 55 years has been a bittersweet experience. I have re-lived extraordinary moments of joy and achievement, as well as moments of despair and failure. I cherish the memory of the many engineers, salesmen, buyers and especially the employees I came to know and with whom I worked. I find great satisfaction in knowing my companies contributed to safety in flight. Supplying the worldwide airline industry enabled me, along with my wife Bea, to travel throughout the world, affording us the gift of meeting people from other cultures, visiting their homes and families and learning more about them, all of which enriched our lives.

I find myself consumed with memory and nostalgia for the whole experience. It has been one great ride. My wish for everyone reading this book, as I said in the preface and as I now urge, *go for it. It can be yours. You, too, can achieve "the impossible dream."*

VALUABLE LESSONS I LEARNED IN 55 YEARS OF BUSTING MY ASS

BELIEVE IN YOURSELF

Believe in yourself. Don't depend on help or well meaning advice from anyone else, family, relatives or friends. Listen and consider what they are saying, but make your own decision. Be thoughtful, don't rush, take your time, think it through and then go for it.

GO DIRECT

Go direct. Don't wait for someone to make a call, make a contact, put in a good word, get you an introduction, etc. Pick up the phone and start calling. The phone is still the most effective instrument of communication. Remember all the times you have waited in a long line in a bank, ticket office, etc. in a hurry only to have a phone ring and have the clerk stop everything to pick up the phone. In my experience, I rarely failed to speak to anyone, regardless of high position, when I tried to reach them on the phone. I have a wild fantasy if I really wanted to get the President of the United States on the phone I could.

LEAD BY EXAMPLE

Be a good, decent person, show interest in each employee, communicate with them, verbalize appreciation for their good work, convey the philosophy that the success of the company is to their benefit as well as to the owners.

From the beginning, sales of our products were the key to our growth and future. That was my job, to motivate our sales force and expand our sales. Rather than remain in the office, I continued to call on customers and travel to wherever we could expand our sales. I reported to our employees the results of these sales trips. I believe our employees appreciated that management was also working diligently to ensure the growth and future of the company.

CREATE A GOOD WORK ENVIRONMENT

My belief regarding employees has always been that they and we spend most of our waking hours on the job, including time coming to and going from the job. Employees are entitled to a workplace that is pleasant, where people are nice, where there is some fun, where there is minimal anxiety, where the physical plant is clean, well lighted, with clean bathrooms, where supervisors treat employees with respect and appreciation and where workers feel comfortable and reasonably happy coming to work.

WAGES, SALARIES, BENEFITS

Always work to have wages, salaries and benefits competitive, but be realistic. Besides competitive wages and salaries, our health benefits were better than those offered by other small companies in our industry. They were as good as, if not better, than some of the major aerospace employers in Southern California.

Very early we instituted a 401(k) plan offering one dollar for every two dollars our employees saved in the plan. Each year we put a sum of money into a pension plan, at times as much as $100,000. Employee participation was based on length of service, wages and salary. A quarterly shipping goal was established. When the company achieved the goal there was a cash distribution to every employee, based on longevity, salary and attendance. The result was very few employees left the company, saving us unlimited amounts of money and time finding and training new employees.

A conservative professional pension management firm managed the pension plan. Besides ensuring loyalty among employees, the pension plan, along with the 401(k) plan, became the major savings for most of our employees. I am proud of the fact that even as a small company we were able to provide these beneficial programs.

GIVE EMPLOYEES RESPONSIBILITY

Be willing to give responsibility to employees. They will respond and it will improve their self image and their appreciation of their job. Compliment their good efforts. If someone makes a mistake, don't go ballistic. We all make mistakes. Never reprimand or criticize an employee in the open workplace in the presence of other employees. Always discuss the situation in the privacy of your office. *Never lose sight of the reality that you need the employee just as the employee needs the job.*

GOOD NEWS, BAD NEWS

From employees you want to hear the good news and you want to hear the bad news. *You must hear the bad news.* It's important your employees understand this and are comfortable telling you the bad news. More times than not there are ways to correct the bad news. Not knowing the bad news is murder. When you finally discover the problem, it is often too late to fix it. In my companies, it was an unforgivable sin not to reveal bad news.

GET TO KNOW YOUR EMPLOYEES

As much as possible, get to know your employees. Converse with them about their families, their health, sports, movies, music, etc. I avoided discussing politics much as I was tempted. I felt I did not want to "pull rank" on anyone's political thinking, but I did encourage them to get involved, to register to vote and to participate in their community activities. We always made donations to school and community activities that were requested of us by employees.

DO NOT LEND MONEY

Do not lend money to employees. Rarely, if ever, will it get paid back. More often it will be to an employee who is likely to leave or be terminated.

TERMINATING AN EMPLOYEE

Terminating an employee was a difficult, even traumatic event for me. On the few occasions when it became necessary, I soon learned I had made a mistake. I waited too long. *Don't wait.* If you know the employee is not really doing the job, forget sentiment and make the change. You owe it to your company.

WATCH YOUR MONEY

Without a doubt, the fact that my companies survived and prospered over 55 years was due to my policy of watching our money very carefully. There are always the regular requirements of wages, salaries, rent, insurance, taxes and unanticipated expenses. Beyond this, do not waste money, do not pay yourself or employees in excess, do not burden the company unnecessarily – in short, be conservative.

Over the years, I witnessed competitors who were not conservative. The owners, on occasion, tapped their company treasuries. When business improved some entrepreneurs threw caution to the wind. On rare occasions an employee succumbed to a higher offer from a competitor and left us. On more than one occasion this same employee asked to come back when there was a downturn in business and those higher wages for which they left us disappeared.

Over the years, by being very careful with our money, we developed an excellent credit rating with our suppliers, a happy relationship with City National Bank, a willingness, at times anxiety, on the part of suppliers to sell to us frequently at preferred prices because they were assured of being paid. We had the ability to compete against many bidders and win competitive bids for material being offered by the government or major original equipment manufacturers. And, of course, we had that good feeling that comes with being financially sound.

DEALING WITH CUSTOMERS

Ours was essentially a phone business. One of my first instructions to a new employee was to our telephone operator. I told her how important her job was, indeed the most important job in the company because she was the first voice of our company a potential customer heard and would immediately influence the customer's first impression of us. I asked her to be reasonably loud, very clear, very definite and *never leave a customer hanging on the other end of the phone*. It all sounds simple and should be taken for granted, but to this day, I'm appalled by the poor performance of telephone operators and receptionists at major corporations. Today's massive use of answering equipment has changed business procedures, but our sales were then and now done mostly over the phone.

Secondly, I reminded our order desk personnel how fortunate we were to be in a business where our products were needed, where our products were designed into aircraft, aerospace, electronic, high speed transportation, theatrical lighting and other commercial uses. When our phone rang, it was because a customer needed and wanted our product.

BE HONEST

From the beginning we did our best to be honest with our customers, our employees and our suppliers. As a supplier to the aircraft and aerospace industries, we were always under pressure to promise early, even immediate delivery of our products. Orders were frequently placed on the commitment to deliver on a specific date. In the competition to get these orders, our competitors frequently quoted earlier dates and received the order, knowing full well they couldn't deliver on time.

It was a cardinal rule in my companies to *level with the customer*, to quote accurate delivery dates and, at times through no fault of ours, if these dates couldn't be met, to contact the customer and advise them of the new delivery date. At times we might have lost the sale, but we retained the customer by our honesty.

DEALING WITH COMPETITORS

I enjoyed dealing with our competitors. In many cases, we grew up together in the industry and had long personal relationships. We recognized we needed each other and there was a desire to be mutually helpful. We had one thing in common – to make a satisfactory living for our families and to build a solid, exciting business.

KEEP A SENSE OF HUMOR

Above all, keep your sense of humor. I can honestly say it has enabled me to deal with the darkest moments in my business life and, of course, the happiest as well. I also found humor to be a great asset and weapon in dealing with customers, suppliers, employees and especially the bank!

LAST LESSON

Don't play golf or tennis with a prospective customer unless you plan on losing to him. Even that can be hazardous. I've played tennis all my life and I'm aware that many tennis players see themselves as better than they are. That probably applied to me. I learned this was true of golfers as well.

On one occasion, a buyer at an important aircraft plant insisted we play golf together after work. Our competitors had been taking him to private clubs, golf tournaments, etc. We needed his business very badly but I was reluctant to play golf with him. My game was poor and I didn't want to spoil his. But he insisted.

I met him at a public golf course after work, bought new balls, tees and paid the course fees. He then suggested we have a bet. I declined, but he insisted. Finally he suggested the bet. "I'll give you a stroke a hole and we'll play for a dime a hole." This was 1960. To my dismay, he was a terrible golfer. By the third hole he owed me 30 cents and wasn't talking to me. So much for his buying electrical connectors from us. It took me nine holes to let him win 10 cents.

The lesson, I repeat – *Never play golf or tennis with a prospective customer unless you plan on losing.* Even that can be a disaster.

EPILOGUE

Everyone's dream is different. Many small companies want to become big companies and many have done just that. I never aspired to getting big. I wanted to build a good company, to become a stable, reliable and profitable company to the industries we served. It worked. Some of my competitors passed me. Observing the working demands on their time and energy, I was content and excited by our own small steps of growth. I wanted to spend as much time with my family as possible. I didn't want the business to take over my life.

There were additional rewards for my approach to business, namely the lasting, enriching experiences and personal relationships with my employees. High among the real joys was my ability to provide employment to so many different people. On some occasions we really didn't need additional help, but they needed the work and we provided the job.

I think of the great years providing summer time employment to my niece Bobbi, now a retired Los

Angeles school teacher; nephews Richard, now Press Secretary to majority leaders in the California State Assembly; Harvey, Professor of Math at Northern Illinois University; Spencer, Professor of Sociology at the University of Anchorage, Alaska; Andrew Jimmy Wood, musician, composer, leader of his own band; my own kids Leni, Ph.D. with a rewarding career as Business Consultant and Coach; Susan, Physician Assistant and our family's "second opinion"; David, Award-winning, hard-working documentary film maker, all of whom at a later date confessed they weren't crazy about the work but were glad they did it.

Then there are our grandchildren: Tara, graduate of Wellesley, third year student at UCLA Law School; Cassie, mother of four and a challenge; Daniel, Haverford College graduate, Discovery Room Science Coordinator of the American Museum of National History in New York; Jesse, Ph.D. candidate at the London School of Economics.

I think of David Haecock, Leni's high school friend who worked three summers, seemingly each summer moving the same boxes from one side of the warehouse to the other. David went on to become an Air Force pilot.

Soon after I started Liberty Aircraft, Henry Chesler, a boyhood friend of mine from Cleveland, visited me. He had migrated to California after World War II and was selling surplus army and navy clothing. Henry (Hank) wanted to go to UCLA to become a teacher. Now married with two children, he was trapped. I suggested to Hank he work at Liberty Aircraft any time he wasn't in school, which he did. Hank completed his work at UCLA and went on to a very distinguished high school teaching career in Los Angeles Public schools.

Paul Jacks, while an employee, during a vacation in Belgium looked up the brother of one of our employees and found him unhappily working in a slaughterhouse. Paul invited him to come to Los Angeles knowing full well I would approve and provide a job and sponsorship.

Steve Von Gelderen started as a warehouseman. After ten years, Steve left, started his own connector business, became very successful and turned over the business to his sons to return to his first love, painting.

When my secretary-employment manager, Sally Hamilton, said there was a Russian Jewish engineer applying for a job, I said "Hire him," sight unseen. Sam had been a diesel engineer in the then disintegrating Soviet Union. Sam became one of Flight connector's most competent and reliable engineers.

We intentionally employed young people with disabilities. They were given jobs for work we required and for which they were capable. On several occasions I went with one of these employees to UCLA Fernald School for disadvantaged students. We paid his tuition and I witnessed his progress in remedial reading.

During the painful loyalty oath Blacklist period of the 1950's, I provided employment to victims of that infamous period in American life. They included high school teachers, social workers, a director of a New York hospital and George Wilner, an elegant man who was a partner in one of Hollywood's leading screen writers agencies. When the studios blacklisted George his agency was dissolved and George was unemployed. With a wife and two children to support, George tried to make a living by buying and selling scrap metal off a truck. One day he came to me and said, "I need to make $100 a week. Do you have a job for me?" Before being blacklisted, George made in excess of $1,000 a week. I had been thinking about starting Electro-Sonic Components. I bought his truck sight unseen and George, with absolutely no experience in managing a warehouse, became a valued employee who helped launch Electro-Sonic Components.

As the Blacklist subsided and mercifully disappeared, these employees were able to return to their former careers. George once again became a successful writer's agent. I'm pleased I was able to help.

I think of Bill Breau, a wonderful young man who had been a pilot for a non-schedule airline that went broke. Bill walked in one warm afternoon and in his quiet way said, "I think I can sell your products." I wasn't looking for another salesman, but I just liked him. Bill took over my territory in Orange County where I had been floundering and ran rings around me with sales and making friends for Liberty Electronics. Now retired after a career of selling connectors, Bill still sings in Barber Shop Quartets. In his seventies, while vacationing in Europe, Bill bought a tuba in a pawn shop and has taught himself to play that neglected instrument.

There was Warren Kleven, our first hard-working Sales Manager. He named his fifth son "Charles Irving Kleven."

His name escapes me, but one summer a young track star at UCLA worked at Spacecraft Components before competing in the Tokyo Olympics as part of the winning U.S. quarter mile relay team.

Not all employment situations were perfect. We were a supplier to Folsom Prison which provided inmates assembly jobs for the electronic industry. The buyer of connectors was a good customer. He was in Folsom having been convicted of auto theft. He told me he could get early release if I could provide him with a job. I confess, I would have preferred he remain in Folsom as he was a reliable buyer of our connectors. Nevertheless, I signed for him and assured him of a job with us. He was a nice young man who was beginning to be a useful employee when, after two months of freedom, he was re-arrested for car theft! We also had to start all over developing a working relationship with the Folsom Prison purchasing department, but it was never the same.

Then there is Eddie Mann, neighbor, electrician, sculptor in stone and wood, banjo player and bagpiper who installed and repaired our companies' machinery and equipment for over two decades. Ed trained our talented warehouse foreman Don Dean on all matters electrical, saving us time and money to this very day. What other company can boast their electrician circled the warehouse at lunchtime playing the bagpipes? Ed is a Renaissance Man. Living two houses away, now retired and in his eighties, Ed is always available to solve electrical and other maintenance problems for our entire neighborhood in the Hollywood Hills. Ed is one of a kind. I treasure our friendship and the help he gave my companies and my family.

Don Dean was our warehouse foreman who never wavered in his belief that all machinery, equipment and maintenance problems could be fixed – which Don did. On occasion I would borrow Don to do some needed repair of matters in my house. I can't say Don saved my marriage, but he sure helped. Besides his work responsibilities, Don made himself and his home available to problem young men who had nowhere to go. Despite a continuing battle with smoking and a back problem, Don played Santa Claus, costume and all, at neighborhood Christmas celebrations. Don is immensely liked by all his fellow employees and made my own companies a better place in which to work.

My thanks to Keith Wiseman, a young man with a big heart. The third of the Wiseman's five children, Keith shot many of the photos in this memoir. Keith responded enthusiastically to any task asked of him. Working his way through practically every department, Keith is now Production Manager of Spacecraft Components. Equally as commendable, Keith repaired obsolete computers and donated them to public schools. Keith is just a real nice person. He, too, helped make Spacecraft Components a better place.

Hoover Louie was and still is my accountant. This memoir could not be complete without my deep thanks and appreciation to Hoover and his dedication to my companies and my family. On the one occasion when we had an IRS review, the IRS officer was, coincidentally, also Chinese. Hoover bemoaned to me, "He's trying to prove he is a smarter Chinaman than I am." I have always been in awe of Hoover for his ability to remember everything, for dealing with minutiae, and for making sure my companies were following the law and encouraging me to be conservative. My grown children now look to Hoover for their accounting and I herein apologize to Hoover because, at times, they must drive him crazy.

I was especially fortunate to have had excellent caring secretaries throughout my career. Sally Hamilton was and is something special. I gladly admit I could never have done much of what you have read in this memoir if it wasn't for Sally Hamilton, my secretary for 28 years. In my many years of working, travel, community activities, sports, even writing this memoir, Sally has been just plain wonderful. She took care of my books, records, checking account and the dozens of niggling things that would drive me crazy. She even followed up on our children's problems and obligations. When we traveled, Sally took care of any and every problem that developed while we were away.

She was and is a whiz at typing, the computer, bookkeeping, understanding our company medical programs, guided our employees through their medical benefits and is a bright, intelligent, concerned woman upon whom all our employees relied and respected. Sally is friendly and attractive. Visitors always enjoyed meeting her. She was a gracious hostess and in every way "set the table" for meeting with our guests. Sally was a major contributor to the success of my companies. She is terrific.

Lastly, my gratitude and thanks to Lynn Tempereau. Lynn rescued me when Sally was no longer available once I left Spacecraft Components. Lynn helped me organize this book, corrected errors, completed the text disk sent to Author's House and encouraged me to stay with it. Best of all, Lynn seems to enjoy the contents of "How to Succeed in Business by Busting Your Ass." Thanks, Lynn.

As I reflect upon the contents of this memoir, I find myself feeling good that I spent most of my working life in and around airplanes. Following the end of World War II, along with millions of returning veterans, I was not certain what I wanted to do to make a living and to provide security for my family. To have found my way into aviation and the aircraft industry made this journey especially rewarding.

I loved flying as a private pilot and as a Navy pilot in World War II. Not to continue flying after the war was an easy decision for me. Piloting a plane is a demanding commitment. Like golf, flying is unforgiving. The difference -- instead of losing a stroke, you can lose your life. To keep up my flying skills would have meant less time with my young and exciting growing family. That didn't keep me from jumping into the co-pilot's seat whenever I found myself in a twin engine with a solo pilot. When I made my flight experience known on several occasions, I was invited into the cockpits of commercial airliners in flight only to realize there was very little in the cockpit that looked familiar. Participating in the ever-expanding worldwide airline community with its never-ending commitment to even better airliners was challenging and rewarding. Being part of the unrelenting need for perfection and security in flight gave my business career something extra. I am still filled with admiration and awe for the men and women pilots who enable millions of passengers to feel safe and secure flying in the commercial airliners everywhere in the world.

Once again, to all hard working men and women who might read this book, who are in business or are thinking of starting a business, I urge you to go for it. It can be yours.

About the Author

Growing up in the Depression of 1929, very early Irving Zeiger began earning money to avoid asking for money from his parents who were struggling to make ends meet. In high school he worked during summers, had a morning paper route which earned him tuition to attend the University of Michigan. He had three jobs while at Michigan. Zeiger graduated the day before the Nazi army marched into the Soviet Union. It was clear the United States was heading for war.

Zeiger enlisted in the Navy Aircorps, became a pilot and served in the Central Pacific. Upon his return he married Beatrice Blau, a wartime romance lasting more than 62 years and counting.

Zeiger entered the Aircraft, Airline, Aerospace Industry in Los Angeles and began busting his ass to succeed. This memoir of 55 years in the industry is a labor of love and bittersweet memories. Zeiger hopes "How To Succeed in Business by Busting Your Ass" will inspire and encourage hard working business men and women and provide them a helpful good read.

Irving Zeiger lives with his wife in Los Angeles, has 3 children, 6 grandchildren and 4 great-grandchildren with whom he is trying to keep up.

Printed in the United States
72521LV00001B/220-300